Kelley Wingate

Reading Comprehension and Skills

Fourth Grade

Credits
Content Editor: Jeanette M. Ritch, M.S. Ed.
Copy Editor: Beatrice Allen

Visit *carsondellosa.com* for correlations to Common Core, state, national, and Canadian provincial standards.

Carson-Dellosa Publishing, LLC
PO Box 35665
Greensboro, NC 27425 USA
carsondellosa.com

ISBN 978-1-4348-0495-8
05-263161151

Table of Contents

Introduction

Reading proficiency is as much a result of regular practice as anything. This book was developed to help students practice and master the basic skills necessary to become competent readers.

The skills covered within the activity pages of this book are necessary for successful reading comprehension. Many of the activities will build and reinforce vocabulary, the foundation of reading comprehension. These activities lead to practice with more advanced comprehension skills. Then, students begin to answer comprehension questions based on specific reading passages.

The intent of this book is to strengthen students' foundation in reading basics so that they can advance to more challenging reading work.

Common Core State Standards (CCSS) Alignment

This book supports standards-based instruction and is aligned to CCSS standards. The standards are listed at the top of each page for easy reference. To help you meet instructional, remediation, and individualization goals, consult the Common Core State Standards alignment chart on page 4.

Leveled Reading Activities

Instructional levels in this book vary. Each area of the book offers multilevel reading activities so that learning can progress naturally. There are three levels, signified by one, two, or three dots at the bottom of the page:

- Level I: These activities will offer the most support.
- Level II: Some supportive measures are built in.
- Level III: Students will understand the concepts and be able to work independently.

All children learn at their own rate. Use your own judgment for introducing concepts to children when developmentally appropriate.

Hands-On Learning

Review is an important part of learning. It helps to ensure that skills are not only covered but internalized. The flash cards at the back of this book will offer endless opportunities for review. Use them for a basic vocabulary drill, or to play bingo or other fun games.

There is also a certificate template at the back of this book for use as students excel at daily assignments or when they finish a unit.

Common Core State Standards Alignment Chart

Common Core State Standards*		Practice Page(s)
Reading Standards for Literature		
Key Ideas and Details	4.RL.1–4.RL.3	5–7, 14–22
Craft and Structure	4.RL.4–4.RL.6	8–13, 18
Integration of Knowledge and Ideas	4.RL.7	17, 20
Range of Reading and Level of Text Complexity	4.RL.10	5–19, 20–22
Reading Standards for Informational Text		
Key Ideas and Details	4.RI.1–4.RI.3	23–46, 50–61
Craft and Structure	4.RI.4–4.RI.6	20, 23–25, 29–31, 41–49, 62–64
Integration of Knowledge and Ideas	4.RI.7–4.RI.9	20, 29–31, 47–49
Range of Reading and Level of Text Complexity	4.RI.10	23–61, 63, 64
Reading Standards: Foundational Skills		
Phonics and Word Recognition	4.RF.3	65–67, 74–85
Fluency	4.RF.4	19, 32–40, 86–91
Writing Standards		
Text Types and Purposes	4.W.1–4.W.3	86–91
Production and Distribution of Writing	4.W.4–4.W.6	86–91
Language Standards		
Conventions of Standard English	4.L.1–4.L.2	92–103
Knowledge of Language	4.L.3	92–103
Vocabulary Acquisition and Use	4.L.4–4.L.6	65–85, 101–103

* © Copyright 2010. National Governors Association Center for Best Practices and Council of Chief State School Officers. All rights reserved.

Character Analysis

Read the story. Then, answer the questions.

Neighbors Need Neighbors

There was an old lady who lived on the edge of town. Everyone referred to her as Granny. Because she kept to herself, she seemed a little different to some. She asked nothing of anyone and did nothing for anyone, except her many dogs. The number of dogs varied daily. Some only came when they were hungry and then left until they returned to eat again. Some knew a good home and stayed.

One day the paper boy noticed Granny's papers had not been picked up for three or four days. The dogs in her yard were thin and moved about slowly. He had not seen Granny for about a week. He wondered if she was all right.

He got off his bike and walked up the steps onto the front porch. He walked around and peered in the windows, but he did not see anything. He opened the front door slightly and called, "Hello! Anyone here?" He listened for a minute. He thought he heard a whimpering sound, so he quickly rode to the closest neighbor's house and called 9-1-1.

When the police arrived they found Granny had fallen and had not been able to move to call for help. The paramedics said Granny needed to go to the hospital where she stayed a few days.

While she was in the hospital, the paper boy came to feed her dogs every day. When Granny came home, neighbors brought food and flowers. Granny was sorry she had not gotten to know her new friends sooner, but was glad she had now "found" them.

1. Circle what Granny's behavior said about her character at the beginning of the story.

   She liked to be alone.   She did not like people.   She was mean.

2. How did Granny's behavior change?

   _____

   _____

3. How did the neighbors' feelings for Granny change?

   _____

   _____

Character Analysis

Read the story. Then, answer the questions.

The Grass Is Always Greener

Once upon a time there was a princess named Priscilla. She had a normal infancy, but when she began to walk her life changed. She was not allowed to go anywhere without being chaperoned by at least five of the royal guards. She wanted to play with other children her age, but her parents did not want her outside the castle walls.

One day she managed to escape the guards' watchful eyes. She ran off to the forest. When she stopped running, she found herself amidst towering trees with hardly any sunlight filtering through their leafy branches. Squirrels ran from tree to tree, a deer sailed by, and from the treetops she heard unusual bird songs she had never heard before.

Suddenly an ugly creature popped out from the shrubbery. He introduced himself as Whiz. He was a wizard and could grant her one wish. Priscilla did not hesitate. She knew just what she wanted. "Oh please, I would like to play with some children outside the castle's walls."

"Not a problem," said Whiz. Immediately she was on a playground in the middle of a dodgeball game. Because she did not know the rules, she was hit with the ball and out of the game. That was not fun. The next game was tag, but she did not know to run so she was always caught. She was therefore always "it." She was exhausted. She was not sure playing with other children was fun. She began to want to go home but did not know exactly where it was.

Luckily the guards who were looking for her came by. When she saw them she jumped for joy. She jumped so high that she landed on the back of a guard's horse and rode home in record time.

Circle how Priscilla felt in each situation.

1. When guards were watching her:	angry	unhappy	contented
2. When she was lost in woods:	frightened	entranced	free
3. When she got her wish:	let down	elated	scared
4. Playing dodgeball and tag:	hurt	playful	discouraged
5. When she saw the guards:	relieved	resentful	encouraged

Character Analysis

Read each paragraph and answer the questions.

Robbie and his dad were walking on the beach on a summer morning. They were talking about how beautiful the beach was. They were looking for signs of animals while the tide was low. Robbie saw something large up ahead on the beach. He and his dad ran toward it. It was a giant whale beached on the sand. Robbie's dad quickly ran to the nearest house so he could call the aquarium.

1. a. Who are the main characters in the story? _____

    b. What is the setting? _____

    c. What is the problem? _____

    d. How do you think the story will end? _____

    _____

Marjie brought her new bike to Danielle's house. Danielle and Marjie took turns riding the new bike. They each rode it around the block several times. Marjie showed Danielle how she could ride her bike without holding the handlebars. Danielle wanted to try, too. Danielle got started and shouted, "Look, no hands!" Then Danielle fell on the sidewalk. She got up right away. Marjie asked if she was all right. Danielle said, "I'm fine, but I think your handlebars are twisted."

2. a. Who are the main characters in the story? _____

    b. What is the setting? _____

    c. What is the problem? _____

    d. How do you think the story will end? _____

    _____

Point of View

> Point of view refers to the person who is telling the story or "speaking." When you write a letter, you are writing in "first person," which includes the words *I, me, my, we,* and *our.* Second-person writing occurs when the author talks about you and yours, and third person includes the words *he, she, they, his, her,* and *their.* In third-person writing, the author does not put himself in the story.
>
> A story can be told from different points of view.
>
> In **first person**, the main character tells the story.
>
> In **second person**, the story is told as though it is happening to you.
>
> In **third person**, a narrator tells the story as if she is watching it happen.

Read each story and circle the point of view.

1. Marcus's family had just moved to a large city from a very small town. He was surprised at how many cars were on the street and how few people said hello when he met them on the sidewalk. In his old town, he had known everyone. He hoped that he would make a new friend on the first day of school. When he saw the crowded hallways as he walked into the building, he felt worried. Then, he thought to himself that with all those people around, he was sure to make a lot of friends.

    first person   second person   third person

2. When my family moved to the big city, I was excited about all of the new activities we could try. I never thought about how crowded it might be. Back home, my neighbors were very friendly. It seemed like I knew everyone in the whole town. I wanted to make new friends in the city, but when I got to school the hallways were so packed I could hardly get to my classroom. I took a deep breath and thought to myself, "With all of these people around, I am sure to make new friends."

    first person   second person   third person

Point of View

Remember, a story can be told from different points of view.

In **first person**, the main character tells the story.

In **second person**, the story is told as though it is happening to you.

In **third person**, a narrator tells the story as if she is watching it happen.

Read each story and circle the point of view.

1. I love gardening. Seeing the little sprouts push up through the ground in early spring makes my heart sing. It can be hard to wait until the plants are fully grown to eat them. My brother likes vegetables, and he enjoys tomatoes in particular. Every year he tries to harvest them too early. At the end of the summer, I gather seeds and plant my crop for the next year. It is fun to see the whole growing cycle.

   first person   second person   third person

2. You love to work in the garden. You especially like seeing the tiny plants first appear through the dirt. Although it is hard to wait, you know that it is better to wait until the plants are fully grown before pulling them up. Your brother is so fond of tomatoes that his mouth begins to water even before they are red. At summer's end, you gather seeds to plant for next spring. You rejoice at the cycle of nature.

   first person   second person   third person

3. Carrie often worked in her garden. She checked the soil every morning to see if any new plants had appeared. Sometimes her brother tried to pick a green tomato, but she always stopped him. She said that it was better to wait until they were ripe. When the summer was over, she planted seeds for a new crop.

   first person   second person   third person

Point of View

Read each story and circle the point of view.

1. Felipe loved to cook. He had been helping his mom and grandma in the kitchen ever since he could remember. One day Mom suggested he cook dinner for Grandma. Felipe was nervous but excited. He wrote a grocery list and asked Mom to take him shopping. They chose fresh vegetables and herbs for a delicious stew. Felipe had watched Grandma cook the stew many times. He thought he could cook it perfectly even without a recipe, as long as Mom was there to answer any questions.

   first person   second person   third person

2. I love to cook. I first started helping my mom and grandma in the kitchen when I was very small. One day Mom suggested I cook dinner for Grandma. I felt excited but also a little nervous. I had never cooked a meal by myself before! Mom and I went to the store with a list of food to buy. She showed me how to choose fresh vegetables and special herbs. I have watched Grandma make stew many times, so I think that I can cook it even without a list of instructions. Mom will be standing by to help just in case.

   first person   second person   third person

3. Your favorite activity is cooking. You have been helping your family in the kitchen since you were a child. One day your mom suggests you cook dinner for Grandma. You are excited but nervous, since you have never cooked a whole dinner by yourself before. You help your mom make a list of things to buy, and then you go to the store. You pick out only the freshest vegetables. Because you have watched Grandma make her special stew many times before, you know you can make it without using a recipe and with only a little help from Mom.

   first person   second person   third person

4. You and your family have just moved to the city. You are surprised at seeing so many cars on the road. In your old town, you felt like you knew everyone. When you drive up to the school, your mother wishes you good luck. You walk into the building and start to look for your classroom. You think that with all these people around, you are sure to make some new friends.

   first person   second person   third person

Point of View

Point of view refers to the person who is telling the story or "speaking." When you write a letter, you are writing in "first person," which includes the words *I, me, my, we,* and *our.* Second-person writing occurs when the author talks about you and yours, and third person includes the words *he, she, they, his, her,* and *their.* In third-person writing, the author does not put himself in the story.

A story can be told from different points of view.

In **first person**, the main character tells the story.

In **second person**, the story is told as though it is happening to you.

In **third person**, a narrator tells the story as if she is watching it happen.

Read each story and circle the point of view.

1. You have been looking forward to the big class picnic for a long time. You and your friends hope to look for wildflowers after you eat lunch. You want to find 10 different kinds of flowers. When the day of the picnic comes, it starts to rain. You are sad at first, but then your teacher reminds you that the flowers need rain to grow. You smile to yourself and think that next time you can try to find 20 different wildflowers.

    first person   second person   third person

2. I had been looking forward to the class picnic for weeks. My friends and I were planning to pick wildflowers after eating our sandwiches. I hoped I could find 10 different kinds of flowers! On the day of the picnic, it was raining. I felt sad at first, but I knew that the rain would help the flowers grow even bigger. The next time we went on a picnic, maybe I could find 20 kinds of flowers!

    first person   second person   third person

Point of View

Remember, a story can be told from different points of view.

In **first person**, the main character tells the story.

In **second person**, the story is told as though it is happening to you.

In **third person**, a narrator tells the story as if she is watching it happen.

Read each story and circle the point of view.

1. Clara ran home from school and checked the mailbox. She was disappointed to find that the mail had not come yet. She was expecting a letter from a special friend. Clara had a pen pal in Korea named Chi. They sometimes sent e-mail to each other, but both girls liked getting letters and funny postcards too. Just then there was a knock at the door. It was the postman! He smiled and handed Clara a letter with a Korean postmark.

    first person   second person   third person

2. I ran home from school yesterday and checked the mailbox. My letter from Chi was not there yet! Chi is my pen pal. She lives in Korea. We sometimes send e-mail to each other, but we both like getting postcards with funny pictures too. I was getting a snack when I heard a knock at the door. It was the mailman, and he had a letter for me! He smiled and said, "Tell Chi I said hello."

    first person   second person   third person

3. You run home from school to check the mailbox. You are disappointed when the letter you are expecting is not there. You are hoping for a letter from your pen pal, Chi, who lives in Korea. You like to send e-mail to each other, but you also like getting postcards and letters in the mail. You hear a knock at the door. It is the mailman, and he has a letter from Chi.

    first person   second person   third person

Point of View

Read each story and circle the point of view.

1. I like rain, and I like sun, but I like snow most of all. Winter is a fun season. I like building snowmen with my brothers and making a fort with snowballs. I like lying in the snow and making patterns with my arms. I help Dad shovel snow off the pathways so that people can walk and drive safely. I also help Mom make cocoa and cookies to warm us up when we come back indoors.

   first person   second person   third person

2. Lupe liked all kinds of weather, but she liked snow most of all. Winter was her favorite season. She liked to build snowmen with her brothers. Sometimes they made a fort with snowballs. Lupe liked to lie in the snow and make patterns with her arms. She helped her dad shovel the sidewalks so that people could walk safely. She also helped her mom make cocoa and bake cookies to warm everyone up when they came back indoors.

   first person   second person   third person

3. You like rain and sun, but you like the snow in winter most of all. You like to build snowmen with your brothers and make forts with snowballs. You like to lie in the snow and make patterns with your arms. You help your father move snow off the sidewalks. Then, you help your mom make cocoa and cookies to warm everyone up!

   first person   second person   third person

4. Dreama and her friends had been looking forward to the class picnic all month long. They wanted to eat sandwiches in the field and then pick beautiful wildflowers. Dreama was hoping to find 10 different kinds of flowers. When she woke up on the day of the picnic, it was raining. Dreama felt sad at first, but she knew that the flowers needed rain to grow. Maybe at the next picnic she could find even more kinds of flowers.

   first person   second person   third person

Theme

Read each paragraph below. Then, circle the theme of the story.

The Hare and the Tortoise

One day a hare was making fun of a tortoise and called him a slowpoke. That made the tortoise mad, so he challenged the hare to a race. Of course, the hare knew he would win. When the hare got far enough ahead, he stopped for a rest and fell asleep. The tortoise plodded along, never stopping. When the hare woke up, he ran as fast as he could to the finish line. However, the tortoise had already crossed it. The moral of the story is . . .

1. a. A lazy hare is fast.

    b. Do not brag.

    c. The slow turtle wins.

The Fox and the Crow

A crow sat in a tree with a piece of cheese it had just taken from an open window. A fox who was walking by saw the crow and wanted the cheese. The fox complimented the crow in many ways. One was to tell the crow how nicely it sang. To prove its voice, the crow opened up his mouth to sing. The cheese fell out, and the fox gobbled it up. The moral of the story is . . .

2. a. Do not let flattery go to your head.

    b. Listen before you sing.

    c. Eat fast so you will not lose your dinner.

The Dog and the Bone

A dog was walking over a bridge carrying a bone. The dog looked into the stream and saw another dog carrying a bigger bone. The dog on the bridge jumped into the water because he wanted the bigger bone. But he dropped his, and there was no other bone. The moral of the story is . . .

3. a. He lost his bone.

    b. The dog was wet.

    c. Think before you act.

Theme

Read the paragraphs below. Then, write the theme of each story.

Because Tammy had to stay after school, she had to ride her bicycle home in the dark. The ride was scary because there were no lights on the dirt road that led to her house. Finally, she could see the lights of her house in the distance, so she pedaled faster. She was not paying close attention to the road when she hit something. Her bike went flying one way and she another. Tammy landed in a soft pile of hay. When she realized she was all right, she climbed up onto the road. Lying in the middle of the road was a box that had broken apart when she hit it. Inside she could see money. She ran the rest of the way home to tell her family what had happened and to make a sign to find the owner of the box.

1. _____

_____

It was snowing hard, and Justin was taking a freshly baked apple pie to Mrs. Harper's house for his mother. Mrs. Harper lived only two blocks from Justin's, but because of the fast falling snow it was difficult for Justin to see any pathways. He trudged on, and snow began to accumulate in large drifts. After a while, Justin did not see anything familiar—just white falling from the sky and white on the ground. He did not know which way to go. He was lost. What seemed like hours passed. Finally, he saw some lights and heard a loud scratching sound. It came closer and got louder. It was a snowplow. The driver asked if he was Justin. Justin was relieved and hopped into the truck's cab. Justin had gone the opposite way of Mrs. Harper's house. When he had not arrived in what should have been a few minutes, she called the city who sent someone out looking for him. Mrs. Harper got her pie, and Justin got a ride home.

2. _____

_____

Theme

Read the story.

Shortcut

We probably should have taken the road home from the baseball park. It was getting dark, though, and we decided to take the shortcut home. I was the oldest and should have made a better choice. I didn't know there would be a train.

The shortcut from the baseball park to home was along the train tracks. After Reggie's game was over, we were excited. The game had gone into extra innings and Reggie's team had won! As we walked, Reggie and I gave each other high fives. Samantha and little Brittany were running to keep up. You know how little sisters are. When we came to the turn for the shortcut, we were so excited and happy that we just took it. We should have stayed on the road.

We walked for about five minutes on the tracks. The sides of the tracks were steep and there were thick bushes and marshy water at the bottom. We stayed on the tracks. Samantha asked how we'd know if a train was coming. I said that we'd feel the tracks rumbling.

It was then that I heard the train whistle far away. I didn't want to worry the little ones, so I just said as calmly as I could, "Let's go back to the road." We turned around and I walked pretty fast. Everyone followed.

Soon we felt the tracks rumbling and I shouted, "Run!" I grabbed little Brittany in my arms and Reggie held Samantha's hand. We ran as fast as we could. Then I could see the headlights and the train blew its loud whistle. We kept running, but I shouted, "Get off the track, NOW!" We jumped off the tracks and slid down the sides. Samantha and Brittany were crying but I could not hear them. The loud train was rushing by us.

After the train went by, we climbed back up the hill. We were all scratched up from the bushes, but no one complained. We were all shaking as we walked back to the road. We didn't have to talk. We all knew we'd never take the shortcut home again.

Choose a theme for the story. Then, give several reasons to explain why you chose this theme.

_____

_____

_____

_____

_____

Referring to Details

Read the story.

Peterson's Pockets

I love pockets! When I pick out a new coat each year, I look for the coat with the most pockets. I especially like hidden pockets. I once had a coat with 12 pockets! I loved that coat.

I also love pants with lots of pockets. I love those pants that have pockets on the side of the leg. I like to put things in my pockets. I put money, bottle caps, cool stones, my yo-yo, notes from my friends, and other stuff I find in my pockets.

My mom doesn't like it that I put stuff in my pockets. Sometimes I forget to take papers out of my pockets before my mom washes my pants. She says it makes an awful mess in the washing machine.

My dad said that long, long ago, pants didn't have any pockets at all! Back then, people wore little pouches that hung from their belts. I would have had to wear a pretty big pouch. My mom says I would have to carry around a suitcase if I didn't have all these pockets.

Did you know that the first pockets on pants were little pouches sewn on the outside of the pants? About 200 years ago, pockets finally were sewn on the inside of pants like they are now.

Someday, I'm going to invent a new place to hide a pocket. Maybe in 200 years, people will be talking about me and my super cool pocket. They will wonder how people ever got along without the "Peterson pocket."

Think of a new place to hide a pocket. Then draw a design to enhance the story. Use labels to describe where the pocket is and what it could hold. Underline the parts of the story that helped you design the pocket.

Referring to Details

Read the story. Then, answer the questions. Underline the parts of the story that helped you answer each question.

Penny's New Glasses

Penny had a hard time seeing the board in class. Rosa sat next to her. Penny asked Rosa to read her the assignment each day. One day, their teacher said, "Penny, I think you should go to the eye doctor."

Penny's mom made an appointment, and, in a few weeks, Penny was waiting in the office of the optometrist. The optometrist called her name and she went into a darkened room. On one side of the room was a large chair with a robot-looking machine in front of it. The doctor told her to sit in the chair. The doctor sat on a small stool on rollers and introduced herself. "I'm Dr. Riley."

Dr. Riley pulled the machine over to Penny. Part of the machine looked like a mask. Dr. Riley told Penny to look through the mask and read some letters on the opposite wall. As Dr. Riley turned some dials, the letters became blurry and then clear. Dr. Riley kept turning dials until Penny said that the letters were very clear and easy to read.

Penny picked out small, round frames that were black. The optician told Penny that her glasses would be ready in about a week. Penny wished she could wear her new glasses home. She was excited.

In a week, Penny went back and picked up her new glasses. She liked the way she looked with her glasses. Her mom said she looked smart.

The next day at school, Penny wore her new glasses. She couldn't wait to show her friends. "It's about time you got glasses," Rosa said. "I'm tired of reading the board for you." Penny laughed when Rosa smiled.

During math, Penny could read the problems on the board. In reading, she had no trouble reading her book. In gym class, Penny made a basket. She felt great about how clear everything was now.

1. Why did Penny's teacher think Penny should go to the eye doctor?

_____

_____

2. How did the eye doctor know how strong Penny's glasses should be?

_____

3. What does an optometrist do?

_____

_____

Referring to Details

Read the story.

Lemonade Stand

Faiza and Emily set up a small wooden table at the corner of Cambridge and Sherman Streets. Faiza set up the supplies. Emily set up two chairs and a large umbrella. Soon they would be open for business.

The girls painted a sign. They lettered the sign carefully: "Lemonade for Sale." They leaned the sign in front of the table.

Then the girls went inside and came back with a heavy cooler. Inside were two pitchers of lemonade and a bag of ice. They also had homemade cookies.

They took one pitcher and set it on the table. Then they put 10 cookies on a plate. They sat down in their chairs and waited.

A car drove by. It didn't stop. A few minutes later, another car drove past. Emily yelled, "Lemonade for sale!" The car kept driving. A third car came by and parked at the neighbor's house. Faiza and Emily both shouted, "Lemonade for sale! Twenty-five cents a cup!" Faiza's neighbor stepped out of the car. She walked over to the lemonade stand.

"Hi, Mrs. Ford," said Emily. "Would you like some lemonade?"

"Sure," said Mrs. Ford. She gave the girls a quarter and drank her cold lemonade. She also bought two cookies and said good-bye.

Emily and Faiza stayed at their lemonade stand for two hours. Many people bought lemonade and cookies. By the time they ran out of lemonade and cookies, they had earned six dollars.

Underline each event in the story. Then, put the events of the day in order by numbering the sentences from 1 to 10.

_____ They carried out the heavy cooler.

_____ Emily set up the chairs.

_____ The neighbor bought some lemonade.

_____ The girls set up the table.

_____ They put 10 cookies on a plate.

_____ They put one pitcher of lemonade on the table.

_____ The girls stayed at the lemonade stand for two hours.

_____ They earned six dollars.

_____ They painted the sign.

_____ Two cars drove by without stopping.

Referring to Details

Read the recipe. Then, follow the directions.

Campfire Walking Salad

Before you pick up your hot dog at the campfire, make a walking salad. You won't need a fork or plate for this salad. Just wrap the salad fixings in a piece of lettuce and carry it in one hand.

Ingredients:

large lettuce leaves   mayonnaise

salted Spanish peanuts   peanut butter

miniature marshmallows   raisins

raw carrot shavings

Directions:

Wash and pat dry several leaves of lettuce. Set out the ingredients on a table. Choose a lettuce leaf and spread mayonnaise or peanut butter on it. Then add the other toppings. Roll up the lettuce like a tortilla and eat.

Draw the steps for making a walking salad. Label the steps and the ingredients. Underline the parts of the recipe that helped you draw each step.

1.

2.

3.

4.

Referring to Details

Read the story. Then, answer the questions. Underline the parts of the story that helped you answer each question.

A Day at the Beach

Erika and Yesenia rode together in the backseat. They were excited because they were going to the beach. Erika had never been to the beach before. She was going with her best friend Yesenia's family.

Yesenia told Erika all about the sand and the waves. She told her about the paddle boat. "I like to paddle out to the deep part and jump in the water," said Yesenia. Erika felt her stomach tighten. She didn't know how to swim. She didn't know that Yesenia was so brave in the water.

The girls had a great time. They played in the water, jumping in the waves and laughing. They built a huge sand castle using buckets and shovels. Erika thought the beach was great!

Then Yesenia's dad called them over to the boat dock. He had the paddle boat ready for them and held two life jackets in his hands. Yesenia ran to the boat, put on her life jacket, and sat down. She smiled and waited for Erika. Erika was very nervous. Yesenia's dad helped her put on her life jacket. Yesenia started pedaling so Erika did too. They were moving quickly across the water. When they were far out in the lake, Yesenia stopped the boat and said, "Last one in the lake has stinky feet!" Yesenia jumped in the water. Erika didn't move. She didn't dare tell Yesenia that she couldn't swim. Would Yesenia laugh at her?

Yesenia watched Erika. Finally she said, "Are you coming in?" When Erika shrugged her shoulders, Yesenia guessed what was wrong. She climbed back in the boat. "Do you know how to swim yet?" she asked kindly. Erika shook her head. Yesenia smiled at her friend and said, "Okay. Let's paddle around some more. Then after lunch, I'll teach you a little bit about swimming." Erika smiled at her best friend. Why had she ever worried about telling Yesenia that she didn't know how to swim?

1. What do you think Yesenia would have done if Erika had told her right away that she couldn't swim?

_____

2. Why do you think Erika waited to tell Yesenia that she couldn't swim?

_____

_____

3. Why do you think Erika didn't know how to swim?

_____

4. What did the girls have fun doing at the beach?

_____

Referring to Details

Read the story. Then, answer the questions. Underline the parts of the story that helped you answer each question.

A Family Hike

We started on the trail early in the morning. The sun was rising in the sky and the air around us was cold and misty. The pine trees looked like arrows pointing our way to the top of the mountain.

My mom and dad each carried a heavy backpack full of food, tents, water, and other things. Ben and I carried packs, too. Mine only had my clothes and sleeping bag in it. I carried a few snacks in my pockets and two water bottles on my belt. Ben carried some food and a cookstove in his pack.

We walked quietly at first. My dad says you don't need words to be part of the forest in the morning. I could hear birds singing and chipmunks moving through the leaves on the ground. There was no breeze so the trees were silent. We walked single file along the trail.

At lunchtime, we stopped by a stream that flowed down the mountain. We could see a small waterfall higher up, but here the water cut through the rock and snaked past flowers and bushes. We took off our shoes and dipped our feet in the water. The sun shone brightly overhead and we all took off our jackets.

I knew better than to ask how much farther we had to go. We would be walking for three days on these trails. We would see many beautiful sights and hear and smell things we don't hear or smell at home in the city. My mom and dad are teachers. Every summer, we take a trip as a family.

We went to bed pretty early because we were all tired from walking. Tomorrow, we will have another long walk. We will reach the top of the mountain tomorrow. My dad says that I will be able to see forever. I think I'll like that. Maybe I will be able to see my friend Gena's house back home. I will wave to her and shout hello. I'll hear the echo and pretend that she shouted back at me. But that is tomorrow, and my dad says that even the night is part of the journey. So I will close my eyes and listen for the owls, the wind in the trees, and the sound of my dad snoring. I love this place!

1. Do you think that there is anyone else in the family who is not on the hike? Explain your answer.

   _____

   _____

2. Do you think the narrator likes this trip? Why or why not?

   _____

   _____

3. Describe the setting.

   _____

Reading about Social Studies: Main Idea

Read the story. Then, answer the questions.

The Aztecs

The Aztec people lived in the area that is now central Mexico. The Aztec Empire lasted from about 1325 to 1521 and stretched from the Pacific Ocean to the Gulf of Mexico. The Aztecs had a strong central government that was headed by a king or emperor. Under him were officials who governed different parts of the empire. The Aztecs enjoyed many foods, including corn or maize, beans, squash, tomatoes, and chili peppers. People in Mexico still eat many of these foods today. The Aztecs built temples that were similar to the Egyptian pyramids but without the pointed tops. On the outside of the temples were steps to the top, where there was a flat area. The Aztec people are known for their pottery and statues. They also made beautiful feathered headdresses, masks, shields, and clothing for their rulers to wear and use. You can find examples of Aztec crafts in museums today.

1. What is the main idea of this story?

   a. The Aztec people lived in the area that is now called Mexico.

   b. The Aztecs had a strong government and made many crafts.

   c. Aztec temples are like the Egyptian pyramids.

2. How long did the Aztec Empire last?

   _____

3. How was the Aztec government organized?

   _____

   _____

   _____

4. How are Aztec temples different from Egyptian pyramids?

   _____

   _____

Reading about Social Studies: Main Idea

Read the story. Then, answer the questions.

World Holidays

People around the world celebrate different holidays. Both Canada and the United States have special days to mark the countries' birthdays. Canada Day is celebrated on July 1, and Independence Day in the United States is celebrated on July 4. On both of these holidays, people may have parades or picnics with their families. Many holidays have special foods associated with them. People may eat turkey on Thanksgiving or chocolate on Valentine's Day. During the Chinese Lantern Festival, people eat sticky rice dumplings. This holiday comes at the beginning of the Chinese New Year, in January or February, and has been celebrated for over 1,000 years! People in many other countries celebrate New Year's Eve on December 31. It is common for people to sing an old Scottish song called "Auld Lang Syne," which can be translated as "for old times' sake." They sing the song to remember the good times of the past and to look forward to more good times in the future.

1. What is the main idea of this story?

   a. Canada Day is celebrated on July 1.

   b. People around the world celebrate different holidays.

   c. Some people eat turkey at Thanksgiving.

2. How are Canada Day and Independence Day similar?

   _____

   _____

3. What are some foods eaten at holidays? _____

4. What festival is held at the Chinese New Year? _____

5. When is the Chinese New Year celebrated? When do other people celebrate the New Year?

   _____

6. Why do people sing "Auld Lang Syne"?

   _____

   _____

Reading about Social Studies: Main Idea

Read the story. Then, answer the questions.

Becoming a U.S. State

There are 50 states in the United States today. The last states to be added were Alaska and Hawaii, in 1959. Most states admitted to the Union after the original 13 were U.S. territories first. To become a state, the people of the territory had to band together with an organized government and then write a state constitution. After the U.S. Congress accepted the constitution, that territory became a state. Areas that might become U.S. states someday include the island of Puerto Rico and the District of Columbia. While people who live in these areas now are U.S. citizens, they have limited voting rights. Puerto Rico has a resident commissioner instead of a senator, and the District of Columbia has a non-voting member of the U.S. House of Representatives. Each of the 50 U.S. states has two senators and one or more representatives in Congress. Some people who live in areas of the United States that are not states believe they need a greater say in Congress. Others would like to keep their independence.

1. What is the main idea of this story?

   _____

   _____

2. What were the last states to be added? When? _____

3. How does a U.S. territory become a state?

   _____

   _____

4. How are U.S. territories different from U.S. states?

   _____

   _____

5. How many members of Congress does each state have? _____

6. Why might someone living in a U.S. territory want statehood?

   _____

Reading about Social Studies: Main Idea

Read the story. Then, answer the questions.

The Mississippi River

The Mississippi River is an important river for trade, recreation, and culture. It runs all the way from the U.S. state of Minnesota down to the Gulf of Mexico and covers 2,340 miles (3,770 km). The name Mississippi comes from an American Indian word meaning "great river." The first European explorer to reach the Mississippi was Hernando de Soto of Spain, who came there in 1541. In 1682 a group of French explorers claimed the river for their country. The city of New Orleans was built near the river in 1718. The United States acquired the area with the Louisiana Purchase of 1803. The Mississippi gained fame with the books of Mark Twain, which described life on the river. Twain, whose real name was Samuel Clemens, worked on a steamboat on the river in the late 1850s. Boats still travel down the Mississippi today, but people also water-ski and fish there. In addition, there are seven National Park Service areas along the river where people can go to enjoy nature.

1. What is the main idea of this story?

    a. The Mississippi River was made famous by Mark Twain.

    b. The Mississippi River was discovered by a Spanish explorer.

    c. The Mississippi River is important in many ways.

2. How long is the Mississippi?

    _____

3. Where did the Mississippi get its name?

    _____

4. Who was Samuel Clemens?

    _____

    _____

Reading about Social Studies: Main Idea

Read the story. Then, answer the questions.

The Field Museum

The Field Museum is a famous museum in Chicago, Illinois. It contains exhibits of animals, plants, and people from around the world. The museum was built in 1893. It was first called the Columbian Museum of Chicago because it contained the objects for the World's Columbian Exposition of that year. Its name was changed in 1905 to honor Marshall Field, who was an early supporter. The Field Museum contains the skeleton of "Sue," the world's largest and most famous Tyrannosaurus rex. Visitors can find out what Sue ate and how she lived. The buildings around the museum include the Shedd Aquarium, which has marine life from tiny sea horses to large sharks, and the Adler Planetarium, where people can find out information about stars and planets. Museum workers conduct research on not only how animals have lived in the past, but how we can save endangered species today. People who visit the museum enjoy seeing the exhibits, but they also like finding out how they can help.

1. What is the main idea of this story?

   a. People like visiting the Field Museum.

   b. The Columbian Museum of Chicago was built in 1893.

   c. The Field Museum has exhibits on many animals, plants, and people.

2. Why was the name of the museum changed?

   _____

   _____

3. Who is "Sue"?

   _____

4. What can you see at the Shedd Aquarium?

   _____

5. What are some things that museum workers do?

   _____

   _____

Reading about Social Studies: Main Idea

Read the story. Then, answer the questions.

Family Trees

Have you ever heard of a family tree? A family tree is not a plant that grows in the park. It is a drawing that shows how everyone in your family is related. The branches of the tree show different parts of your family. Before you begin to create a family tree, you should find out the names of as many family members as you can. Research this by asking your relatives. Then, begin to draw your tree. Write your name in the middle. Next to your name, write the names of your siblings. Above your name, write the names of your parents or stepparents. Above each of their names, write the names of their parents. You may want to draw a picture of each person or use photographs. Building the tree together can be a fun activity for the whole family. You may find out you are related to someone famous!

1. What is the main idea of this story?

_____

2. What do the branches of a family tree show?

_____

3. Why should you talk to relatives about the family tree?

_____

_____

4. Where do you write your name on a family tree?

_____

5. What goes above each name on a family tree?

_____

6. What might you discover as you make your family tree?

_____

Reading about Social Studies: Main Idea

Read the story. Then, answer the questions.

The Economy

You may have heard your family or a newscaster discuss the economy. The economy is a system in which goods and services are exchanged for money. Goods are things that are produced, such as books and clothing. Services are things people do for each other. For example, a teacher provides the service of educating students, and a police officer provides the service of keeping the community safe. Sometimes people provide a service that produces a good, such as a cook who prepares a meal that you can eat. People pay money for goods and services. When you give money to a producer of goods, she can purchase materials to make more goods. When you give money to a service provider, he may pay for more training to do his job better. They can also use the money to pay for basic items such as food and shelter. When newscasters report that the economy is strong, it means that most people are happy with the amount of money, goods, and services they have.

1. What is the main idea of this story?

   a. Newscasters often talk about the economy.

   b. Sometimes the economy is strong, and other times it is weak.

   c. The economy is a system in which goods and services are exchanged for money.

2. What are goods?

   _____

3. List two examples of goods.

   _____

4. What is a service?

   _____

5. List two examples of service providers.

   _____

   _____

Reading about Social Studies: Main Idea

Read the story. Then, answer the questions.

Citizen Rights and Responsibilities

People who are citizens of a country have certain rights that belong to them. These rights are sometimes listed in the laws of that country. In Canada and the United States, citizens over the age of 18 are given the right to vote. Citizens also have the right to a fair trial and the right to speak freely about what they believe. They can practice any religion they want to, and they have the right to gather peacefully to exchange ideas. They have the right to ask their government to change laws that they think are wrong. With these rights come responsibilities too. People should obey the laws of their country. They should respect the opinions of others, even if they disagree with them. They should help others in their community and try to protect their environment. It is important to remember that all citizens are part of a large community and that everyone deserves to be treated fairly.

1. What is the main idea of this story?

   a. All citizens of a country have rights and responsibilities.

   b. Citizens have the right to vote.

   c. Everyone should be treated fairly in a community.

2. Where can you find a list of citizens' rights? _____

3. How old must citizens be to vote in Canada and the United States? _____

4. What are three rights in Canada and the United States?

   _____

   _____

5. What are three responsibilities in Canada and the United States?

   _____

   _____

6. Why is it important to treat all citizens fairly?

   _____

   _____

Reading about Social Studies: Main Idea

Read the story. Then, answer the questions.

City Services

Cities provide many services to people who live there. The mayor and city council, who are elected by the citizens of that city, make the laws that everyone must follow. They also meet to discuss community issues, such as whether to build a new recreation center. Other city employees include police officers and firefighters. These people work to keep everyone in the city safe. Other city services are at the library, where the public can check out books, and at companies that provide water and electricity. Some cities have special programs for the people who live there, such as reading clubs at the library or computer classes for senior citizens. It takes many services to make a city work. Some people like to give back to their community by doing volunteer work. They might teach swimming lessons or offer to pick up litter in the parks. When everyone in a city works together, it can be a great place to live.

1. What is the main idea of this story?

   _____

2. Who elects the mayor and city council? _____

3. What do the mayor and city council members do?

   _____

   _____

4. Name three employees who work for the city.

   _____

5. What kinds of programs might a city have?

   _____

6. How can people help their community?

   _____

7. In what ways do you help your community?

   _____

Reading about Social Studies: Critical Thinking

Read the story. Then, answer the questions.

Tipi

For thousands of years, people have lived on the Great Plains of the United States and Canada. The Great Plains is a huge expanse of flat, grassy land with few trees. Many different animals used to roam on the plains. The groups of people who lived there would travel around and follow the animals to hunt. They needed homes that they could tear down and set up pretty quickly. Many Plains tribes, such as the Blackfoot, Sioux, and Cheyenne, built tipis to use as homes.

The first step in making a tipi was to find and prepare the poles. It took 15 poles to make just one tipi. The poles for the frame had to be long and straight. The best trees for this purpose were willow, pine, and cedar. The branches and bark were cut off so they did not poke holes in the tipi cover. When the people traveled with their homes, the poles dragged on the ground. The poles wore out and had to be replaced every year or two.

To prepare the buffalo hides, the women worked together on many steps. First, they scraped and cleaned the inside and outside of each hide. Then they soaked the hides with water to soften them. Next, they sewed as many as 14 hides together in the shape of a half circle. They cut a hole for the door and created smoke flaps. Finally, they fitted the cover over the frame and lit a fire inside. The smoke from the fire helped to preserve the skin. Some tipis were decorated with designs and symbols.

In the late 1800s, life on the Plains changed a lot. Many roads and cities began to fill the area. The buffalo were almost all gone. Many of the Plains people were forced to live on reservations. They no longer lived in tipis. Still, the tipi remains an important part of Native American culture today.

1. What are some tribes that live in the Great Plains?

_____

2. Describe the poles needed to make a tipi.

_____

_____

_____

3. How did women prepare buffalo hides?

_____

_____

_____

Reading about Social Studies: Critical Thinking

Read the story. Then, answer the questions.

The *Titanic*

The *Titanic* was one of the finest ships ever built. It was built to be comfortable and luxurious. What was life like on this expensive ship that only sailed on one voyage?

There were three levels of tickets. The most expensive tickets were for "first class." The next level was for "second class." The least expensive tickets were for those traveling in "third class" or "steerage."

The 329 "first-class" passengers had four decks on which to move around. They had cabins with sitting rooms. They could also visit with friends in several different lounges, restaurants, and dining rooms. They had a gym, a pool, a Turkish bath, a library, and beautiful sunny decks. Dinners consisted of many courses. First-class passengers could choose their meals from a menu. They ate at tables decorated with china plates, crystal, and fresh flowers. Some people wrote about what the ship was like. It was even fancier than what most rich people had at home.

The 285 "second-class" passengers were treated like the first-class passengers on other ships. They had nice cabins, but they were small. They ate a four-course meal each evening. They could also go on deck to walk around or sit in the sun. They did not have the restaurants, gyms, and other special rooms of the first class.

The 710 "third-class" passengers had space in the noisy rear of the ship below second class. There were only 220 cabins in "steerage." These cabins were used for families. The other passengers slept in large rooms. The men were in one room and the women were in a second room. The steerage sitting room was a large, plain room with benches and tables. Third-class passengers had to take turns eating in a dining room that sat only 473 people at a time. A ticket told them when to eat. If they missed their time, these passengers went hungry until the next meal.

Read the words of each passenger. Write whether the passenger is first-class (1), second-class (2), or third-class (3).

_____ "I love my room. I have a beautiful bedroom with a private sitting room."

_____ "My favorite meal is dinner when we have a delicious four-course meal."

_____ "We swam for hours in the pool."

_____ "In the evening, we sit on benches in the only room we all share. We play music and dance."

_____ "I love to sit on the deck in the sun. My brother likes to play in the small cabin."

_____ "We had to eat a little fast so the next group of people could come in and eat."

Reading about Social Studies: Critical Thinking

Read the story. Then, answer the questions.

The *Mayflower*

Imagine leaving behind your home and all your things to sail across the ocean to a new world where there are no towns and no homes. This is what the passengers of the *Mayflower* faced in their journey from England to America in the year 1620.

The *Mayflower* traveled for 66 days across the unpredictable Atlantic Ocean. The ship carried 102 passengers and nearly 30 crew members. The passengers were the people who were riding on the boat from England to America. The sailors, or crew, were the people who worked on the ship. The crew planned to return to England once the passengers were settled.

Travel was difficult in rough weather. Passengers ate oatmeal, hard biscuits, dried fruit, rice, and salted beef brought with them from England. Many of the passengers became seasick during the trip. Occasionally, when the weather was calm, they would go up on deck to get fresh air and stretch their legs. The sailors preferred them to stay below and out of their way.

Every sailor was busy with the job of maintaining the ship. Some sailors climbed high on the mast to the lookout. Others put the sails up or down and repaired torn sails. Some sailors steered the boat. Others cooked for the crew in the forecastle. Many of the sailors helped to keep the boat clean. The sailors were paid well, but it was hard work.

When the ship landed in the Plymouth harbor, the passengers started the difficult task of settling in. They needed to build homes and get ready for the coming winter. Even the children had to work hard.

As soon as the passengers were settled, the crew of the *Mayflower* began the long, hard journey back to England.

1. Why do you think the sailors were paid so well? List three reasons.

   _____

2. Why didn't the passengers go up on deck very often?

   _____

3. How was the trip on the Mayflower different from a trip on a big ship today?

   Food: _____

   How the ship was powered: _____

   _____

4. On a separate sheet of paper, write a paragraph explaining why you think life will be hard for the passengers in their new land.

Reading about Science: Main Idea

Read the story. Then, answer the questions.

Comets

Comets are objects that look like dirty snowballs flying through space. They have tails of dust that may be over 6 million miles (10 million km) long. Besides the tail, a comet has a nucleus, or center, made up of a closely packed ball of ice and dust. Surrounding the nucleus is a cloud of water and gases referred to as the coma. People can see comets only when they pass close to the sun. As they get closer to the sun, some of the ice in the nucleus melts, forming the long tail. Some comets appear after regular periods of time. Halley's Comet, named after Edmond Halley, the person who first predicted its return, passes through the solar system every 76 years. It was last seen in 1986 and will appear again in 2062. Earth is in no danger from comets. When the planet passes through the comet's tail, small pieces of rock called meteors fall into the atmosphere. Most of these are burned up in the mesosphere. They appear during a meteor shower as shooting stars.

1. What is the main idea of this story?

   a. Halley's Comet is very famous.

   b. Comets are objects from outer space made up of dust and ice.

   c. Comets are not dangerous to Earth.

2. Describe the parts of a comet.

   _____

   _____

3. What happens as a comet gets closer to the sun?

   _____

4. Who was Edmond Halley?

   _____

5. What is a meteor?

   a. a comet that passes by every 76 years

   b. ice from the comet's nucleus

   c. a small piece of rock from space

Reading about Science: Main Idea

Read the story. Then, answer the questions.

Plant Parts

Plants have many parts. You can see some of them, and there are parts you cannot see. The plant begins with the root system underground. It sends out long, thin roots into the soil to gather water and minerals. The part of the plant that grows out of the ground is called the stem. The stem moves water and minerals from the soil up into the leaves. Sunlight helps the leaves make more food, which is moved to other parts of the plant. The leaves also produce the oxygen in the air we breathe. Some leaves have only one broad, flat area connected to the stem. Others have many leaflets, or slim, needle-like parts. Many plants have flowers at the top of the stem. The petals of a flower help attract bees and butterflies, which bring pollen from other flowers. The pollen helps the flower make new plants the next year. Some plants produce fruit. When the seeds in the middle of the fruit are planted, a new plant can grow.

1. What is the main idea of this story?

    a. A plant's root system is underground.

    b. Plants have parts such as roots, leaves, and petals.

    c. Bees and butterflies like flowers.

2. How does the root system help the plant?

    _____

3. What do leaves need to make food for the plant?

    _____

4. Describe two ways that leaves can look.

    _____

    _____

5. How do the petals of a flower help the plant?

    _____

6. What happens when seeds from fruit are planted?

    _____

Reading about Science: Main Idea

Read the story. Then, answer the questions.

Endangered Species

Many species of animals around the world are endangered today. This means that there are very few of them left. Species sometimes become endangered through loss of habitat, as when a wilderness area is changed by building a city there. They may also become endangered when people hunt them for food or for their skin. Many countries keep lists of the species that live there and are endangered. People can work to protect these species' environments from further loss. They can also move animals to zoos or nature preserves to try to increase their numbers. When they think it is safe again, they will reintroduce the animal to its native habitat. The alligator was once on the U.S. Endangered Species List because many people liked to make shoes or purses from its tough hide. After a law was passed making it illegal to kill alligators, the number of alligators in the wild increased. In 1987, it was removed from the list. The alligator is an endangered species success story!

1. What is the main idea of this story?

_____

2. What does it mean for an animal to be endangered? _____

3. How do species become endangered?

_____

4. How do people work to protect species?

_____

_____

5. When do people take animals back to their native habitat?

_____

6. Why was the alligator removed from the U.S. Endangered Species List?

_____

_____

Reading about Science: Identifying Details

Read the paragraphs. Underline the sentence in each paragraph that tells its main idea. Highlight the details to support each main idea.

Primates

One reason to classify animals is to determine which ones are related to one another. Usually such classification is achieved by studying the skeletons and skins of the animal. Have you ever wondered to which animal you are related?

Monkeys and apes belong to a group called primates. (The word primate comes from a Latin word meaning first.) Monkeys and apes are called primates because they have complex brains. They are the most intelligent of all animals. Human beings are also classified as primates. Monkeys and apes have large brains like us and use their front limbs as hands. Monkeys, apes, and humans can think and use tools.

Early primates probably ate insects, but they also ate leaves and fruits. The chimpanzee is the most human looking of the primates. Although it eats mostly fruits, it will eat vegetables. It has even been seen eating insects and killing and eating small animals. Chimpanzees use sticks to get honey from a honeycomb or to dig ants and termites from their nests.

Reading about Science: Identifying Details

Read the following passage. Then, follow the directions.

Rattlesnakes

Rattlesnakes are poisonous reptiles whose home is anywhere from southern Canada in North America to Argentina in South America. There are 31 species of rattlesnakes. A large majority of them live in the southwestern United States and in Mexico.

A rattlesnake has excellent eyesight and a great sense of smell. Its forked tongue senses a combination of smells and tastes. It has ears but cannot receive outside sounds since an external and middle ear cavity are missing. It has an inner ear that enables it to detect ground vibrations.

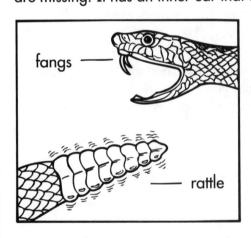

fangs

rattle

The rattlesnake has two long teeth called fangs. The fangs inject a bitten animal with the snake's poison, called venom. Rattlesnakes hunt and eat rodents, small birds, lizards, and frogs whole. Because snakes digest food slowly, a rattlesnake may not hunt for several days.

The rattlesnake's rattle is probably its best known feature. It is a series of interlocking segments that vibrate whenever the tail shakes. When you hear its rattle, you do not want to go any closer.

Circle all of the facts that complete each sentence.

1. Rattlesnakes are _____.   good pets   reptiles   poisonous

2. Rattlesnakes have _____.   fangs   different colors   no ears

3. Rattlesnakes eat _____.   rodents   small birds   humans

4. Rattlesnakes live in _____.   Mexico   South America   Alaska

5. Rattlesnakes can _____.   talk   see   smell

Reading about Science: Identifying Details

Read the story. Then, answer the questions.

How Earthquakes Happen

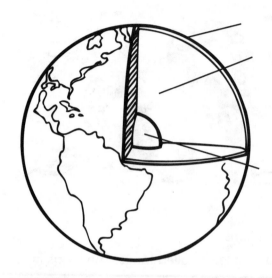

Earth consists of four layers. The center is the core. The core consists of two parts: the inner and outer cores. The inner core is solid, and the outer core is liquid. The mantle surrounds the core. It is solid, hot rock. The crust covers the mantle. As the mantle moves around on the fluid of the outer core, it cracks the crust. The area of crust that breaks is known as a fault.

The cracked crust results in pieces of crust called plates. A plate is a large section of Earth's crust. The Earth's crust is made up of large and small plates. The plates are continually moving. Sometimes they bump, crunch, or move apart from each other. This movement eventually causes an earthquake.

In an earthquake, the ground moves back and forth and up and down. This movement may last seconds or a few minutes. When the shaking occurs, tall buildings can sway, pictures may fall off walls, and dishes may rattle. Fires may break out if the shaking causes underground gas lines to break. Lives may be lost. Earthquakes can cause a lot of damage.

1. Label the layers of Earth on the picture above.

2. What is a crack in the crust called? _____

3. Why might fires occur during an earthquake? _____

   _____

4. What causes an earthquake? _____

   _____

5. What damage can an earthquake do? _____

   _____

   _____

Reading about Science: Explaining Concepts

Read the story. Then, answer the questions.

Vaccinations

Some people go to the doctor for shots called vaccinations. Vaccinations can protect people and animals from diseases. The first vaccination was developed by Edward Jenner, who was looking for a way to prevent smallpox in the late 1700s. Vaccinations work by injecting a dead or weak part of the disease into a person or animal. The body makes antibodies to fight the disease, and the person or animal then becomes immune to that disease. This means that they will not develop the disease, or they will have only a very mild form of it. The most important animal vaccine is for the disease rabies. Many cities require that people vaccinate their pets so that none of them will catch the disease from a wild animal. Some people build natural antibodies to the diseases in their area. If you visit another country, you may be required to get a vaccination for a disease that exists in that country. People who live there might have natural antibodies to the disease, but a visitor might not. Vaccinations can help build antibodies to diseases with which you would not normally come into contact.

1. What disease was the first vaccination developed to prevent?

_____

2. How do vaccinations work?

_____

_____

3. What does it mean to become *immune* to something?

   a. to get a shot at the doctor's office

   b. to have little chance of getting sick from a disease

   c. to visit another country

4. Why might you need a vaccination when you visit another country?

_____

_____

Reading about Science: Explaining Concepts

Read the story. Then, answer the questions.

Ecosystems

All living plants and animals live in ecosystems. An ecosystem can be as large as Earth or as small as a puddle. A lizard might live in a desert ecosystem. A whale would live in an ocean ecosystem. In an ecosystem, all of the living things, such as plants and animals, and nonliving things, such as the soil and the weather, work together. Changing even one thing will affect the other parts of the ecosystem. For example, if the ecosystem where frogs live becomes polluted, the frogs may become sick. If something happens to the frogs, then the animals that eat them, such as snakes, will not have enough food. If there is a fire in a forest, then the mosses on the forest floor will not have shade to grow in. The ecosystem will change from one with large trees and plants that need cool temperatures to one with plants that do well with more sunlight. People must try to protect the ecosystems in which they live. It is important to remember that even if you cannot see every organism in the ecosystem, everything is connected.

1. What is an ecosystem?

   _____

2. Name three types of ecosystems.

   _____

3. What happens if one thing is changed in an ecosystem?

   _____

4. What might happen if frogs in an ecosystem disappeared?

   _____

5. What might happen after a forest fire?

   _____

   _____

   _____

Reading about Science: Explaining Concepts

Read the story. Then, answer the questions.

Biofuels

Gasoline is used in cars, and oil is used to heat many homes. Biofuels have similar uses, but they are made from things like vegetable oil, which can be recycled and used again. Diesel is a type of fuel similar to heating oil. Diesel fuel is used in cars and trucks. Biodiesel, most of which is made from soybean oil, burns more cleanly than diesel. It can be used in diesel engines without having to add any special parts. Biodiesel produces less pollution, so it is better for the environment. Gasoline is known as a fossil fuel, which means that it comes from layers deep under the earth that are made up of plants and animals that lived millions of years ago. Biofuel comes from plants we grow today, so it is a renewable resource. Some biofuels are created from restaurants' leftover grease that was used to make foods such as french fries or fried chicken. Instead of throwing this grease away, people are finding ways to power their cars with it.

1. What are biofuels?

   _____

   _____

2. Why might people choose to use biodiesel rather than diesel fuel?

   _____

3. What is a fossil fuel?

   _____

4. What is a renewable resource?

   _____

5. What are some things used to make biofuels?

   _____

6. What do you think about using biofuel? Write your response below.

   _____

Reading about Science: Vocabulary

Read the story. Then, answer the questions.

Volcanoes

Volcanoes are special mountains that sometimes shoot a hot liquid called lava into the air. Beneath a volcano is a pool of molten, or melted, rock. When the pressure underground builds up, the liquid is forced upward and out of the cone, or top, of the volcano. The liquid inside the volcano is called magma, but when it reaches the surface it is referred to as lava. A lava flow may travel down the sides of the volcano and over the land for several miles. As lava gets farther from the top of the volcano, it cools down and moves more slowly. Volcanic eruptions can be very harmful. Ash is sent into the air and can make it difficult to breathe. Rocks and lava from the eruption can flatten everything around the volcano, including forests and towns. Most volcanoes in the United States are located along the West Coast and in Hawaii and Alaska. The world's largest active volcano is in Mauna Loa, Hawaii. Another region of the world with many volcanoes is in the Pacific Ocean. This area is known as the Ring of Fire.

1. What is the main idea of this story?

    a. The Ring of Fire is located in the Pacific Ocean.

    b. Volcanoes shoot lava into the air and can be very dangerous.

    c. Lava flows can reach for miles around a volcano.

2. What is the cone of the volcano?

    a. the top, where lava shoots out

    b. the pool of molten rock underneath the earth

    c. the area around the volcano

3. What is the difference between magma and lava?

    _____

    _____

4. How can volcanoes be dangerous?

    _____

    _____

    _____

Reading about Science: Vocabulary

Read the story. Then, answer the questions.

Simple Machines

When you think of the word machine, you may picture a car engine or a lawnmower. These machines have many moving parts. Simple machines are tools that people use to make their work easier. They have very few parts. Instead of electric power, they use the energy of people to work. One simple machine is a lever. A lever is a board that rests on a turning point that makes it easier to lift things. A seesaw is a lever. Students on a seesaw use the board to make it easier to lift each other. Another simple machine is an inclined plane. To incline something means "to lean it against something else." An inclined plane is a flat surface that is higher on one end than the other. A ramp is an inclined plane. You might use a ramp to wheel a cart up to a curb instead of having to lift it. A slide is another inclined plane. Simple machines can make our lives easier in ways that are simple yet important.

1. What is the main idea of this story?

    a. Car engines and lawnmowers have many parts.

    b. A seesaw is a type of simple machine.

    c. Simple machines can make our lives much easier.

2. What do simple machines use instead of electricity?

    _____

3. What is a lever?

    _____

    _____

4. What does it mean to *incline*?

    a. lean at an angle

    b. use a simple machine

    c. play on a seesaw

5. What is an inclined plane?

    _____

Name _____

Reading about Science: Vocabulary

Read the story. Then, answer the questions.

Atoms and Molecules

Everything around you is called matter—from your chair to your clothes to your family. Matter is made up of atoms and molecules, which are very tiny building blocks. Atoms make up chemical elements, such as the oxygen in the air you breathe. Atoms are combined to create molecules, such as the water you drink. Atoms are composed of even smaller particles called protons, neutrons, and electrons. A proton has a positive charge, an electron has a negative charge, and a neutron has no charge. The protons and neutrons stay together in the nucleus, or middle, while the electrons orbit, or move around, the atom. The number of protons determines the type of atom that is formed. Hydrogen is the simplest atom. It has only one proton. Oxygen has eight protons. Together, hydrogen and oxygen can form a molecule of water. Each water molecule has two hydrogen atoms and one oxygen atom. A glass of water contains too many molecules to count!

1. What is the main idea of this story?

   _____

2. What are two examples of atoms?

   _____

3. What does *orbit* mean?

   _____

4. Describe the differences between protons, neutrons, and electrons.

   _____

   _____

5. Why is hydrogen the simplest atom?

   _____

6. What is a water molecule made up of?

   _____

Reading about Science: Visual Aids

Read the following information. Then complete the chart.

Mollusks

Mollusks belong to a large family of invertebrate animals. Animals that belong to this group usually have soft, one-sectioned bodies that are covered by hard shells. A person walking on a beach might find discarded shells. We think of them as seashells, but once an animal lived in them.

Biologists divide mollusks into seven groups called classes, but only some of them have hard protective shells. Gastropoda is one class of mollusks. Most gastropods have a single, coiled shell. Included in this class are slugs, snails, and whelks. They can be found on the beaches of the Atlantic and Pacific Oceans in North America.

Bivalves is another large class of mollusks. The shells of bivalves are two shells hinged together at one end or along one side. The animals that call these shells home include clams, mussels, and scallops. They, too, can be found on both coasts of North America.

A third class of mollusks are chitons. Their bodies are covered by eight shell plates that look like a turtle's shell. Merten's chiton, northern red chiton, and mossy mopalia are all included in this class. Chitons live in shallow rock pools. They are found along the Pacific Ocean from Alaska to Mexico.

	gastropods	bivalves	chitons
What do their shells look like?			
Where can they be found?			
List mollusks included in each class.			

Reading about Science: Visual Aids

Read the story. Then, follow the directions.

The Brain

The brain is an organ of the body that controls almost everything the human body does. It is divided into three parts. Each part controls different bodily functions. The three parts are the medulla, the cerebellum, and the cerebrum.

The medulla is located where the spinal cord enters the head. It takes care of involuntary actions. Involuntary actions do not require any decision making. They happen without any thought. Breathing, digestion, and elimination are examples of involuntary actions.

Voluntary acts demand some instruction. Brushing one's teeth, dressing, or turning a somersault are examples of voluntary actions. The cerebellum is the part of the brain that controls bodily movement.

The largest part of the brain is the cerebrum. It controls voluntary mental operations such as the senses, muscles, speech, thinking, remembering, learning, and deciding. The cerebrum is divided into two equal parts called hemispheres. The hemispheres are covered by a layer of nerve cells called the cortex. There are many centers located in different areas of the cortex that send and receive messages. Each of the operations the cerebrum controls is located in a different center.

Write each word or phrase in the diagram to show the main idea and its supporting ideas.

a. involuntary actions

b. parts of the brain

c. cerebellum

d. medulla

e. cerebrum

f. voluntary movements

g. voluntary mental operations

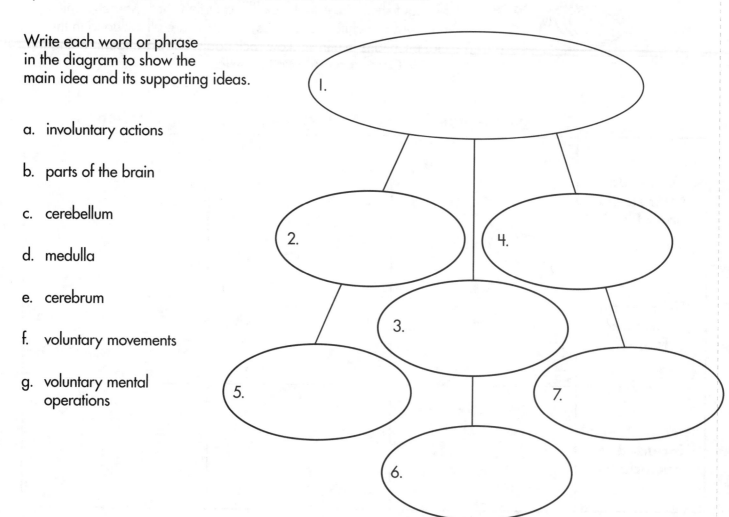

Reading about Science: Visual Aids

Read the story and diagram. Then, answer the questions.

Dinosaurs lived long ago—about 60 million years ago. Today all that is left of them are their fossils, bones, and footprints. But what does 60 million years mean to someone your age? A geologic time scale was developed by scientists that illustrates the periods in Earth's history. It can help those of us living today gain some perspective about the time involved in the development of life on Earth.

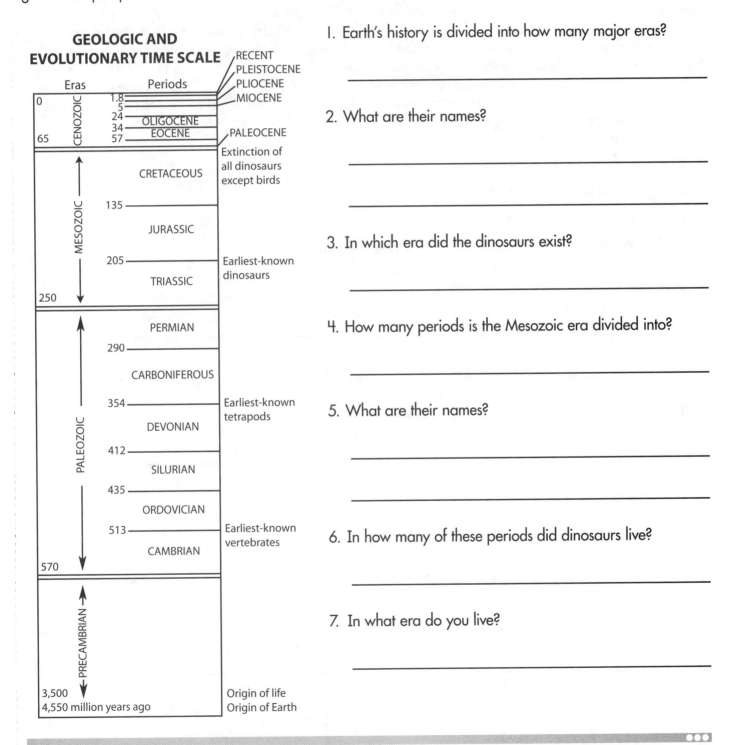

1. Earth's history is divided into how many major eras?

   _____

2. What are their names?

   _____

   _____

3. In which era did the dinosaurs exist?

   _____

4. How many periods is the Mesozoic era divided into?

   _____

5. What are their names?

   _____

   _____

6. In how many of these periods did dinosaurs live?

   _____

7. In what era do you live?

   _____

Reading about Symbolism

Read the story. Then, answer the questions.

Smiley Face

You have probably seen a bright yellow smiley face in an ad or on a sign. Some people even wear them on T-shirts! The smiley face was created in 1963 by an artist named Harvey Ball. Ball was asked to come up with a symbol for an insurance company to use. The company wanted employees to feel cheerful about working for the company when they saw the smiley face. Ball drew something very simple and made the background yellow because it reminded him of the sun. Soon, the symbol became so popular that thousands of people outside the company were wearing smiley face buttons. In the 1970s, the smiley face was put on T-shirts, coffee mugs, and bumper stickers. It has brought a smile to many people's faces around the world. Today, people sometimes use smiley faces in their e-mails to represent different feelings. Harvey Ball probably never thought his symbol would still be used over 40 years later.

1. What is the main idea of this story?

   a. The smiley face is still used today.

   b. Harvey Ball created the smiley face.

   c. The smiley face is a simple symbol that has been around for a long time.

2. Why was the smiley face created?

   _____

   _____

3. Why did Harvey Ball make the background yellow?

   _____

4. How was the smiley face used in the 1970s?

   _____

5. How do people use the smiley face today?

   _____

   _____

Reading about Symbolism

Read the story. Then, answer the questions.

Colors

   Colors can symbolize different things. When you see the color orange, you might feel happy because it reminds you of a sunny day. It might make you feel warm. When you see the color blue, you might feel calm because it makes you think of a still lake. It might make you feel cool to think of swimming in the water. When you see the colors green, brown, and blue together, you might think of the beauty of nature. These colors are used on world globes. Colors can also be used to alert us to danger. Fire trucks are red so that people will notice them and move out of the way. Stoplights use colors to tell cars whether to move. A red light signals to stop, a green light signals to go, and a yellow light signals to yield, or to slow down and be more careful. Pay attention to the colors around you. They might help you in ways you do not expect.

1. What is the main idea of this story?

   a. Colors can mean many different things.

   b. A still lake might make you feel calm.

   c. Pay attention to the colors around you.

2. What does the color orange make you think of?

   _____

3. What does the color blue make you think of?

   _____

4. Why might green, brown, and blue make you think of nature?

   _____

5. Why are fire trucks red?

   _____

6. What do the colors on a stoplight mean?

   _____

   _____

Reading about Symbolism

Read the story. Then, answer the questions.

Political Parties

Political parties are groups of people who feel the same way about one or more issues. Each party may work to elect several candidates to office, from the president down to the city mayor. Political parties often use symbols to represent them. When people see that symbol, they will think of the party. The donkey was first used in a political ad to represent President Andrew Jackson, who was a Democrat. Donkeys can be smart and courageous. The U.S. Republican Party symbol is the elephant. Elephants are known for their strength and intelligence. Both of these parties use red, white, and blue—the colors of the U.S. flag. Many of the Canadian political parties have maple leaves as part of their logos, or designs. The maple leaf appears on the Canadian flag, so this shows that the parties are tied to their country. Political parties in Great Britain use different symbols. The Labor Party uses the rose (the national flower), the Conservative Party uses the oak tree (for strength), and the Liberal Democrats use a dove (for peace).

1. What is the main idea of this story?

   _____

2. What are political parties? _____

3. Why does the Democratic Party use a donkey?

   _____

4. Why does the Republican Party use an elephant?

   _____

5. Why might a political party use symbols from its country's flag?

   _____

6. What are some symbols used by British political parties? _____

7. What is an issue you feel strongly about?

   _____

Reading about Symbolism

Read the story. Then, answer the questions.

Country Flags

Each country of the world uses a different flag. The flag tells something special about that country. It may have colors that are important to that country's people. It may have a picture of an important animal. The flag of the United States has 13 stripes and 50 stars. The stripes represent the original 13 colonies, and the stars stand for the 50 states in the country today. The flag of Canada has a maple leaf. There are many maple trees in Canada. The red leaf is shown on a white band between two bands of red.

1. What is the main idea of this story?

   a. The Canadian flag has red and white areas.

   b. A flag may have animals on it.

   c. Flags tell something special about a country.

2. Why does each country have its own flag?

   _____

3. What things might you find on a flag?

   _____

4. What do the stripes and stars represent on the U.S. flag?

   _____

   _____

5. What does the maple leaf mean on the Canadian flag?

   _____

Reading about Symbolism

Read the story. Then, answer the questions.

Coats of Arms

A coat of arms is a special design used by a family or another group to show something special about that group. Coats of arms were used by knights in the Middle Ages to identify themselves. This design might be passed down through a family. A coat of arms often has an area called a "shield" in the middle. The shield may have different shapes or colors. Around the shield, there may be animals such as lions or eagles. Above the shield, there may be a special saying, such as "Knowledge and Honor." Countries sometimes use coats of arms as well. The Great Seal of the United States has many of the same elements as a coat of arms. It shows a bald eagle holding 13 arrows in one claw and an olive branch with 13 leaves in the other. The number of arrows and leaves stand for the 13 original states. The seal is used on important papers. It also appears on the U.S. one-dollar bill.

1. What is the main idea of this story?

   a. A coat of arms often has a shield on it.

   b. Coats of arms can stand for a family or another group.

   c. The Great Seal appears on the U.S. dollar bill.

2. What is a coat of arms?

   _____

   _____

3. How were coats of arms used in the Middle Ages?

   _____

4. What different things might appear on a shield?

   _____

5. What might appear above the shield? _____

6. Describe the Great Seal of the United States.

   _____

   _____

Reading about Symbolism

Read the story. Then, answer the questions.

What Are Symbols?

Symbols are things that stand for other things. We use symbols such as letters to stand for the sounds we make when we speak. The words made up by the letters stand for ideas. A symbol can tell how you feel about something. Your school might have a symbol such as a lion or a panther that stands for its teams. When you think of that animal, you feel pride in your school. Some symbols are used to stand for bigger things. The flag is a symbol of your country. A TV station might use a symbol to show the channel its programs are broadcast on. You can also see symbols in many buildings. Symbols help you know which restroom to use and which doors are accessible to people that use wheelchairs. These symbols are used as a kind of shorthand so that you can see the picture and quickly know what it means. Symbols are important in our everyday lives.

1. What is the main idea of this story?

   _____

2. What are symbols?

   _____

3. Where might you see a symbol?

   _____

4. Why might a school team use an animal as a symbol?

   _____

5. Why might a TV station use a symbol?

   _____

6. Why are symbols important?

   _____

7. Design your own symbol to represent yourself on a separate sheet of paper.

Reading about Symbolism

Read the story. Then, answer the questions.

Birthday Symbols

Many people recognize their birthdays by doing something special, such as inviting their friends over or having a family dinner. There are also special symbols that stand for the different months of the year, such as flowers and gemstones. Each of these also has a meaning connected with it. For example, the flower for March birthdays is the daffodil. This yellow flower represents happiness and friendship. The flower was chosen because it blooms during that month. Gemstones are another way of recognizing different birthday months. These pretty, sparkling rocks are polished and used to make jewelry. People might wear earrings, a necklace, or a pin with their birthstone in it. The gemstone for January is the deep red garnet stone. May's birthstone is an emerald, which is bright green. The most famous birthstone is probably the diamond, which stands for the month of April. On your next birthday, remember your special flower and gemstone too.

1. What is the main idea of this story?

    a. Stones and flowers always stand for the same thing.

    b. The daffodil is the flower for March.

    c. Each month has a special flower and stone.

2. What does the daffodil stand for?

    _____

3. How are birthday flowers chosen?

    _____

    _____

4. What are gemstones?

    a. polished rocks used in jewelry

    b. special kinds of flowers

    c. stones that are dull and gray

5. What do garnets and emeralds look like?

    _____

Reading about Symbolism

Read the story. Then, answer the questions.

Flowers to Remember

Many countries have special days to remember different people. These days have special flowers connected with them as well. Mother's Day is celebrated in Canada and the United States on the second Sunday in May. Many people give carnations to their mothers on Mother's Day. The flower for Grandparents' Day, which is celebrated on the first Sunday after the U.S. Labor Day, in September, is a forget-me-not. These flowers are small and blue and have a yellow center. Another special day is Veterans Day. On this U.S. holiday, people honor the soldiers who have served in the military. In Canada, this holiday is Remembrance Day, because people *remember* those who have served. Both of these holidays are observed on November 11 every year. In Canada, people wear poppies on their coats. Poppies are red flowers with a black middle. The flowers stand for the poppies that bloomed over a French battlefield during World War I.

1. What is the main idea of this story?

   a. Some people wear poppies on their coats.

   b. Different flowers are worn on special holidays.

   c. Special days help us remember different people.

2. When is Mother's Day celebrated in the United States and Canada?

   _____

3. What flowers are used for Mother's Day and Grandparents' Day?

   _____

   _____

4. What does *remembrance* mean? _____

5. When are Veterans Day and Remembrance Day celebrated? _____

6. What do the poppies worn on Remembrance Day stand for?

   _____

   _____

Reading about Symbolism

Read the story. Then, answer the questions.

Symbols of Canadian Provinces

While Canada has many national symbols, such as the loon and the maple leaf, each of its provinces also has special symbols to represent it. Many of them have provincial plants, animals, and mottoes, or sayings. The province of Newfoundland and Labrador even has its own song! Alberta's official flower is the wild rose, and its bird is the great horned owl. Its motto is "strong and free," and its provincial fish is the bull trout. New Brunswick's flower is the purple violet. Its bird is the black-capped chickadee, and its tree is the balsam fir. Nova Scotia's official animal is a dog called the duck-tolling retriever. Its name means that it is good at finding ducks. Manitoba's bird is the great gray owl. Its official animal is the bison, and its tree is the white spruce. The province's motto is "glorious and free." Each province also has its own flag to show something about the history of that area.

1. What is the main idea of this story?

_____

2. What is a *motto*?

_____

3. What is special about the province of Newfoundland and Labrador?

_____

4. List the provincial flowers for two Canadian provinces.

_____

5. What does a provincial flag tell you about that province?

_____

6. Develop your own motto. Write it below.

_____

Reading about Symbolism

Read the story. Then, answer the questions.

The Loon

The loon is the state bird of Minnesota (United States) and the provincial bird of Ontario (Canada). Loons can be found in the northern part of the United States and throughout most of Canada. A loon is about the size of a large duck and has a dark head and checkered gray and white feathers. Loons dive for fish in lakes as deep as about 200 feet (61 m) under the surface. They can swim for long distances underwater. Loons fly south to Mexico in the winter and come back north when the ice melts in the spring. In 1998, the Canadian postal service issued a special stamp worth one dollar that had a picture of a loon on it. The loon also appears on the Canadian dollar coin, which was introduced in 1987. This coin is often called the loonie. The Canadian two-dollar coin, introduced in 1996, features a polar bear. People call this coin the toonie.

1. What is the main idea of this story?

    a. Loons are special birds in Canada.

    b. Loons dive for fish underwater.

    c. The Canadian dollar coin is called the loonie.

2. Which U.S. state and Canadian province honor the loon?

    _____

3. Where are loons found?

    _____

    _____

4. What does a loon look like?

    _____

    _____

Reading about Symbolism

Read the story. Then, answer the questions.

U.S. State Symbols

The United States has many national symbols that represent liberty and freedom. Each U.S. state also has its own symbols, including state animals, flowers, and flags. The state of Washington has a picture of George Washington, the first U.S. president, on its flag. The state fruit is the apple, and the state vegetable is the Walla Walla sweet onion, which grows in the city of Walla Walla. Louisiana has a pelican, the state bird, on its flag. The state reptile is the alligator. Alaska's flag shows a pattern of stars known as the Big Dipper. The state fish is the king salmon, and the state mineral is gold. Ohio's state insect is the ladybug. The state tree is the buckeye, and the state beverage is tomato juice. Texas is known as the Lone Star State because its flag has a single star on it. The state plant is the prickly pear cactus, and the state flower is the bluebonnet. Each state's symbols can tell you a lot about the plants and animals that live there.

1. What is the main idea of this story?

    a. National symbols represent liberty and freedom.

    b. U.S. states have many different symbols.

    c. The state tree of Ohio is the buckeye.

2. What are the state bird and reptile of Louisiana?

    _____

    _____

3. What does the Alaska flag look like?

    _____

4. Why is Texas called the Lone Star State?

    _____

5. What do a state's symbols tell you about it?

    _____

    _____

Reading about Symbolism

Read the story. Then, answer the questions.

Animal Symbols

Animals can mean different things to different people. To one family, a squirrel might be just a pest in the yard, but to another, a squirrel might serve as a reminder to put away food for the winter. A lion represents strength and courage, but it also stands for the country of Great Britain. It appears on the country's official coat of arms and reminds people of King Richard the Lionheart. The eagle stands for freedom, strength, and courage. It appears on the Great Seal of the United States and is also important in many American Indian cultures. Sports teams often choose an animal to represent them on the playing field. The team members remember their animal's qualities, such as speed and power, when they are playing. Some cars are also named after animals, such as a mustang or a ram, so that people will think the cars are as fast or as strong as those animals.

1. What is the main idea of this story?

   _____

   _____

2. How might people see squirrels differently?

   _____

   _____

3. What does the lion stand for? _____

4. What does the eagle stand for? _____

5. Why might a sports team choose an animal to represent it?

   _____

   _____

6. Why are some cars named after animals?

   _____

Compare and Contrast

Read the diagram. Then answer the questions.

WHAT HAVE YOU READ?

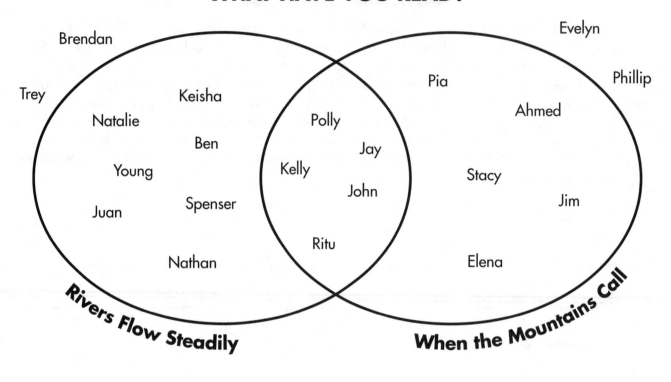

1. How many children have read *Rivers Flow Steadily*? _____

2. How many children have not read *Rivers Flow Steadily*? _____

3. How many children were questioned? _____

4. Which children have not read either book? _____

_____

5. How many children have read *When the Mountains Call*? _____

6. Which children have read both books? _____

_____

Compare and Contrast

Read the passage. Then, follow the directions.

Elephants

There are two kinds of elephants living today, the Indian elephant and the African elephant. The Indian elephant is smaller, stands about ten feet tall, and weighs about four tons. It has smaller ears, a high forehead, and only one lip at the end of its smooth trunk. There are five nails on each of its front feet and four on each hind foot. Only the male has small tusks. The Indian elephant is usually the one seen in zoos. The African elephant is around eleven feet tall, and weighs about six tons. Its ears are big, and its forehead is sloped. Its front feet each have four nails, and the hind feet each have three nails. Also, its trunk is ringed, and its tusks are large.

Compare the two kinds of elephants by filling in the chart below. First, write the names of the two kinds of elephants on the top lines. Then fill in their vital statistics. If the information was not given in the article, fill in the blank with "not given."

1. Elephants   _____   _____

2. Height: _____   _____

3. Weight: _____   _____

4. Ears: _____   _____

5. Forehead: _____   _____

6. Lips: _____   _____

7. Skin on trunk: _____   _____

8. Tusks: _____   _____

9. Nails: _____   _____

Compare and Contrast

The men in the passage below have had similar and yet different lives. Read the passage about them. Then, underline three facts in blue that show the differences between the players. Underline three facts in red that show their likenesses.

Michael Jordan and Kareem Abdul-Jabbar

Michael Jordan grew up in North Carolina. His father built a basketball court in the backyard for all his children to use. Michael enjoyed all sports, but basketball was his favorite. Jordan tried to make his high school's varsity team, but the coach thought he was too short. However, by his junior year he had grown and sharpened his basketball skills, and he made the high school team. The rest is history: getting a scholarship to the University of North Carolina, winning the national championship for the University, helping the U.S. Olympic basketball team win a gold medal, and becoming a Chicago Bull. Michael Jordan broke many National Basketball Association (NBA) records and received several Most Valuable Player (MVP) awards. He retired from basketball and tried baseball, but after two years away from basketball, he returned and set even more records.

Kareem Abdul-Jabbar was born Ferdinand Lewis Alcindor, Jr. He was born and raised in the New York City area. Early on, he had a passion for music and baseball. He played in Little League and was a pitcher for his junior high school. Not until the summer between first and second grade did he first pick up a basketball. In eighth grade he led his junior high to win the district championship. Lew made the high school varsity team his freshman year and the rest is history: leading his high school to record-setting winning streaks, receiving a scholarship to the University of California at Los Angeles, and leading the team to three titles while receiving three MVP awards. During his college years he changed his name to Kareem Abdul-Jabbar. He also boycotted the 1968 Olympics. He and other U.S. athletes decided a boycott would send a message about racism in the U.S. After college he was drafted by the Milwaukee Bucks and then traded six years later to the Los Angeles Lakers. For both teams he had personal and team successes. He was voted MVP five times. He was the NBA's leading scorer and led both teams to national championships.

Determining Meaning

> Some words have more than one meaning. You can tell which meaning is being used from the context of the sentence.
>
> Examples: The ticket taker **admitted** Alan into the theater after the movie started. Here, admitted means permitted or allowed.
>
>   Nancy **admitted** she had not done her homework. Here, admitted means confessed or acknowledged.

Circle the correct definition for the underlined word.

1. Perry was wearing an <u>olive</u> shirt with a tan skirt and socks.

   a fruit

   a color

   an evergreen tree

2. The police arrested the driver at the scene of the accident and <u>booked</u> him for reckless driving.

   entered charges against

   made reservations

   printed pages bound together in a volume

3. The horse <u>bolted</u> from the barn during the heavy rainstorm.

   a rod to fasten a door

   a roll of cloth

   darted off; dashed

4. After the long hike, Mike saw the beginning of a blister on his <u>sole</u>.

   the only one

   a flat fish

   the bottom of the foot

5. Mary stood <u>erect</u> and went for shelter when she heard the tornado warning.

   straightness in bodily posture

   build

   set up or establish

6. We walked several blocks before we were able to <u>hail</u> a taxi.

   icy precipitation

   signal

   greet with enthusiasm

7. Mom had to <u>tramp</u> through the snow to reach the mailbox.

   a person with no fixed home

   to step heavily

   shovel

8. The <u>light</u> in the corner of the room flickered just before it burned out.

   not heavy

   lamp

   brightness

Determining Meaning

At times you may not recognize a word in a sentence or know its meaning, but there are ways to figure it out. One is by its part of speech. Example: The carpet's colors **harmonize** with those of the walls and furniture. Decide what part of speech the underlined word is, what function it has in the sentence, and what it actually means.

Another way is to use the other words in the sentence. Example: The team was **forlorn** after losing the game. The other words tell you that the team was sad.

Use context clues to choose the correct word. Write it on the blank.

1. _____ is one of Tom's favorite subjects. (Astronaut, Astronomy, Atmosphere)

2. He _____ liked to follow the movement of the stars. (especially, establish, exceptionally)

3. Tom was delighted when his family gave him a _____ for his birthday. (telegram, telephoned, telescope)

4. Part of his birthday present was also to go camping with his father to a park where

   _____ were good for stargazing. (constellations, conditions, conjunctions)

5. When the night came for Tom to go to the park, he took the necessary equipment with which to make his

   _____. (observes, orbits, observations)

6. Tom saw several _____ including Orion and the Dippers. (consultants, constellations, confirmations)

7. He drew pictures of what he saw and recorded their positions using a _____. (compass, confess, congress)

8. He had a wonderful time and asked if his father would take him on another _____ to observe the stars. (explore, expedition, experience)

Determining Meaning

Space Science

The Space Age began in 1957 when the United Soviet Socialist Republics (U.S.S.R.) <u>launched</u> the first satellite named Sputnik I. Though the satellite was very small, the importance of its mission <u>transformed</u> how the world is able to look at space. Sputnik I was the first object to go beyond Earth's <u>atmosphere</u>. Since then thousands of satellites have been launched, mostly by the <u>former</u> U.S.S.R. and the United States. Today the satellites are much larger and heavier. Some weigh several tons, and their <u>payloads</u> have a purpose related to the design of each satellite's <u>mission</u>. Today's satellites are designed to perform different tasks, including exploring Earth and space, observing the weather, improving communications, and assisting the military.

Until the Space Age there were <u>theories</u> about space, but they could not be proven. They could only be <u>evaluated</u> from observations and using instruments on the ground. The atmosphere that surrounds Earth <u>distorts</u> the way the stars really look because of the substances within the atmosphere. By putting satellites beyond Earth's atmosphere, scientists can get a better picture of distant stars and perhaps the <u>universe</u>.

Use context clues to choose the meaning for each underlined word above. Write the underlined word next to its definition.

1. the layers of gases surrounding Earth _____

2. initiated; released _____

3. determined; tested _____

4. a specific task _____

5. changed _____

6. twists normal shape _____

7. before in time _____

8. beliefs; analyses of a set of facts _____

9. everything in an entire space system _____

10. loads carried by a satellite necessary for the flight _____

Multiple Meanings

Many words have more than one meaning. Sometimes you can figure out the correct meaning by seeing how the word is used in a sentence.

Read the sentences below. Circle the correct meaning for the underlined word in each sentence.

1. She offered a concrete suggestion on how to create a plan.

   a. made of cement   b. solid

2. The large candle gave off a brilliant light.

   a. very smart   b. very bright

3. My goal is to become a famous scientist someday.

   a. ambition   b. points scored in some sports

4. The patch of pumpkins grew very well.

   a. area of land   b. scrap of cloth

5. When a storm is coming, my cat acts very odd.

   a. number that is not even   b. unusual

6. It is sometimes hard to be patient.

   a. calm about waiting   b. ill or injured person

7. It took several tries at walking before the baby felt stable on her feet.

   a. steady   b. place where horses are kept

Multiple Meanings

Read the sentences below. Circle the correct meaning for the underlined word in each sentence.

1. The principal idea in the essay is that recycling is important.

   a. school leader   b. main

2. Mom suggested I channel my energy into playing basketball.

   a. focus   b. body of water

3. The fish was covered in slimy scales.

   a. small, thin plates   b. instruments used for weighing

4. The *Titanic* began to sink after it hit an iceberg.

   a. place to put dishes   b. go underwater

5. I checked out a volume from the library.

   a. book   b. how loud something is

6. Stefan bought a bolt of cloth to make curtains.

   a. metal used to fasten   b. roll of fabric

7. Writing a thank-you note is a nice gesture.

   a. hand motion   b. idea

8. Eleanor's view is that riding a bike is fun.

   a. opinion   b. sight

Multiple Meanings

Read the sentences below. Circle the correct meaning for the underlined word in each sentence.

1. The sailor took the <u>vessel</u> out to sea.

    a. part of the body that moves blood   b. ship

2. The football player <u>weaved</u> through the other people on the field.

    a. moved in a zigzag manner   b. sewed cloth

3. The <u>plot</u> of the film was unusual.

    a. storyline   b. area of land

4. The <u>beam</u> from the powerful flashlight lit every corner.

    a. plank of wood   b. light

5. Please do not <u>tread</u> on the flowers.

    a. step heavily   b. part of a tire

6. The mayor <u>proposed</u> a new plan to control traffic.

    a. suggested   b. asked someone to marry

7. The <u>glare</u> from the sun hurt our eyes.

    a. frown   b. bright light

8. Larry was the <u>sole</u> winner of the spelling bee.

    a. part of the foot   b. only

9. All of his <u>limbs</u> were sore after he completed the race.

    a. tree branches   b. arms and legs

Multiple Meanings

Read the sentences below. Circle the correct meaning for the underlined word in each sentence.

1. We hailed a cab to go home after the play.

   a. ice from the sky   b. called for

2. The tone of the film was joyful.

   a. sound or vibration   b. mood

3. Do you know who coined the phrase "to each his own"?

   a. turned into money   b. made up

4. My brother hatched a plan to finish his homework and see the movie too.

   a. thought of   b. came out of an egg

5. Many members of royalty have titles like "emperor" or "queen."

   a. words that come before names   b. phrases that describe a book

6. We are having a major test on Friday that covers three chapters.

   a. person in the armed forces   b. important

7. Paulo was not present when the guest speaker came to school.

   a. gift   b. in attendance

Multiple Meanings

Read the sentences below. Circle the correct meaning for the underlined word in each sentence.

1. My stepdad says my mom is the anchor of our family.

   a. strong support   b. metal weight on a ship

2. The referee gave the signal to begin the game.

   a. motion   b. traffic light

3. Mom made sure the picture frame was level before hanging it on the wall.

   a. even on both sides   b. flat and smooth

4. As the tomatoes grew bigger, they began to swell.

   a. excellent   b. grow in size

5. Mrs. Chin used a baton to conduct the band.

   a. direct or guide   b. behave in a certain way

6. It took me a few hours to recover after the long hike.

   a. put new cloth over something   b. feel better

7. I wrote an outline before starting my essay.

   a. drawing around   b. list of important points

8. Milk will not last very long if you leave it outside in hot weather.

   a. remain fresh   b. the end of something

Multiple Meanings

Read the sentences below. Circle the correct meaning for the underlined word in each sentence.

1. My aunt often works the night <u>shift</u> at her job.

   a. period of time   b. to change or move

2. We stopped to pay a <u>toll</u> when we crossed the bridge.

   a. slight charge   b. sound of a bell

3. The Olympic swimmer reached his <u>peak</u> during his best event.

   a. mountaintop   b. best point of performance

4. Lan's pants had a <u>trace</u> of dirt on them.

   a. small mark   b. to draw around something

5. Every time a truck goes by, it <u>jars</u> our living-room windows.

   a. pots   b. rattles

6. I kept <u>dwelling</u> on my teacher's kind words after class.

   a. thinking about   b. living place

7. Olivia thought she could <u>spy</u> a squirrel in the treetop.

   a. secret agent   b. glimpse

8. A U.S. senator's <u>term</u> of office is six years.

   a. word or phrase   b. length

9. Before my dog was trained, his behavior was too <u>rough</u>.

   a. rowdy or forceful   b. bumpy or jagged

Word Analysis Skills: Prefixes

> A **prefix** comes at the beginning of a word.

Look at the words below. Write new words by adding *re-* before each. The prefix *re-* means "to do something again." Use the new words to fill in the blanks in the sentences below.

claim _____

consider _____

fuel _____

turn _____

tell _____

cycle _____

1. After school is out, I will _____ to my house for the day.

2. After speaking to her coach, Josie will _____ her decision to quit the team.

3. Mom stopped at the gas station to _____ her car on her way to work.

4. Our family tries to _____ products so that less trash goes into the landfill.

5. My neighbor came to _____ his lost dog.

6. Uncle Joe likes to _____ his favorite joke over and over again.

Word Analysis Skills: Prefixes

Look at the words below. Write new words by adding *un-* before each. The prefix *un-* is used to make something into its opposite. Use the new words to fill in the blanks in the sentences below.

aware   _____

important   _____

safe   _____

lock   _____

like   _____

cover   _____

affected   _____

1. It can be _____ to ride your bicycle barefoot.

2. Kirby was _____ that the plan for the weekend had changed.

3. I used my key to _____ the door.

4. The parade was _____ by the dark clouds.

5. After I make my bed, I will _____ my pillow.

6. That painting is _____ any other I have seen.

7. Dad says it is _____ whether I am tall or short.

Word Analysis Skills: Prefixes

Look at the words below. Write new words by adding *re-* before each. The prefix *re-* means "to do something again." Use the new words to fill in the blanks in the sentences below.

fill _____

build _____

wire _____

new _____

read _____

do _____

appear _____

write _____

1. An electrician will _____ the fan to make it work.

2. After the teacher looks at our rough drafts, we will _____ our papers.

3. The flowers in the garden are gone, but they will _____ next spring.

4. I need to _____ my membership before it expires.

5. Jim had to _____ his poster after it got wet in the rain.

6. Dad will _____ the doghouse now that our puppy has grown.

7. I enjoyed the book so much that I am going to _____ it.

8. I asked Mom if I could _____ my drink.

Word Analysis Skills: Prefixes

A **prefix** comes at the beginning of a word.

Look at the words below. Write new words by adding *un-* before each. The prefix *un-* is used to make something into its opposite. Use the new words to fill in the blanks in the sentences below.

usual _____

limited _____

common _____

friendly _____

certain _____

able _____

1. When I was walking to school this morning, I saw an _____ sight.

2. It is _____ to have snow here in October.

3. Her uncle was _____ whether he could attend the play.

4. If it is raining tomorrow, we will be _____ to run the relay.

5. At first, the girl seemed _____ but it turned out she was just shy.

6. We had _____ trips to the buffet during the all-you-can-eat lunch.

Word Analysis Skills: Prefixes

Look at the words below. Write new words by adding *under-* before each. The prefix *under-* means "to be below another thing" or "to not have enough of something." Use the new words to fill in the blanks in the sentences below.

stand   _____

taking   _____

cooked   _____

brush   _____

water   _____

foot   _____

cover   _____

1. The detective went _____ to solve the mystery.

2. This project is a large _____ but I know we can handle it.

3. The diver explored the _____ caves.

4. My dog always seems to be _____ when I am trying to walk.

5. Uncle Kieran thought the bread was ready to eat, but it was _____.

6. I _____ how to do the most difficult math problems.

7. Dad cleared away the _____ from our backyard.

Word Analysis Skills: Prefixes

Look at the words below. Write new words by adding *after-* before each. The prefix *after-* means "to come after or later than something." Use the new words to fill in the blanks in the sentences below.

noon _____

effect _____

taste _____

image _____

glow _____

thought _____

shock _____

care _____

1. After the operation, the nurses provided _____ to the patient.

2. The _____ of running the race was that I was tired the next day.

3. After looking at the bright stadium lights, the player saw an _____ each time he blinked.

4. The _____ from the fireworks lit the sky for a moment.

5. After an earthquake, a city may have an _____.

6. Adding fresh strawberries was an _____ but they made the pancakes taste great!

7. The spicy food left a strong _____ in my mouth.

8. Every _____ I play with my friends down the street.

Word Analysis Skills: Prefixes

> A **prefix** comes at the beginning of a word.

Look at the words below. Write new words by adding *be-* before each. The prefix *be-* means "on or around" or "to cause something to happen." Use the new words to fill in the blanks in the sentences below.

fore _____

side _____

low _____

come _____

cause _____

ware _____

1. Jamal said he liked the movie _____ it was funny.

2. The sign said to _____ of snakes on the trail.

3. There are roses growing _____ my bedroom window.

4. It is important to study _____ a test.

5. Cherie hopes to _____ an author one day.

6. Pattie sits _____ her best friend, Kara.

Word Analysis Skills: Prefixes

Look at the words below. Write new words by adding *over-* before each. The prefix *over-* means "to go above or have too much of something." Use the new words to fill in the blanks in the sentences below.

flow _____

due _____

night _____

sight _____

looked _____

heat _____

cast _____

1. The bucket started to _____ after it had rained all week.

2. If you _____ the roast, it will be too dry.

3. My friends and I are planning an _____ slumber party.

4. When the clouds hid the sun, the sky was _____.

5. My library books will be _____ if I do not turn them in today.

6. The mistake in that book was an _____.

7. Miss Gomez _____ my name the first time she read the list.

Word Analysis Skills: Prefixes

Look at the words below. Write new words by adding *out-* before each. The prefix *out-* means "to go beyond." Use the new words to fill in the blanks in the sentences below.

come   _____

last   _____

look   _____

put   _____

spoken   _____

run   _____

wit   _____

numbered   _____

1. Tina was able to _____ everyone else in the race.

2. The presidential candidates each had a different _____ on taxes.

3. Their team _____ ours by five people.

4. My aunt is quite _____ about her ideas on recycling.

5. I hope to _____ the other students during the spelling bee.

6. In the story, the clever hen was able to _____ the fox.

7. Jared was pleased with the _____ of his baseball game.

8. Our _____ has increased since we started working as a team.

Word Analysis Skills: Suffixes

A **suffix** comes at the end of a word.

In the sentences below, choose the word with the correct suffix for each blank.

1. My puppy is learning to _____. Her _____ is very good. (behave, behavior)

2. We asked our teacher to _____ our project. She thought it was a great idea and

   gave us her _____. (approve, approval)

3. Raul could not believe his good _____. He thought he was _____
   to be chosen as the lead in the class play. (fortunate, fortune)

4. My aunt is known for her _____. She can _____
   even the most cluttered closet. (organization, organize)

5. Please _____ your interest in the club by signing the list. Your name is an

   _____ that you want to join. (indicate, indication)

6. My sister and I do not look very _____. Our one _____ is that we
   both have blonde hair. (similarity, similar)

Word Analysis Skills: Suffixes

In the sentences below, choose the word with the correct suffix for each blank.

1. My best _____ is Consuela. She is _____ to everyone. (friend, friendly)

2. Steve would like to be a _____ He wants to _____ either social studies or art. (teach, teacher)

3. The painting was a _____ work of art. Its _____ was known throughout the world. (magnificence, magnificent)

4. The principal will make an important _____ this afternoon. She will

   _____ the winners of the school poster contest. (announcement, announce)

5. Earth is part of the vast _____. Gravity is a _____ scientific law. (universe, universal)

6. Shanika's piano playing will _____ the crowd. Their _____ will be great. (astonishment, astonish)

7. Our soccer team was _____. Our coach led us to _____. (victory, victorious)

Word Analysis Skills: Suffixes

In the sentences below, choose the word with the correct suffix for each blank.

1. I have great _____ for my mother. Many other people _____ her too.
(admire, admiration)

2. Juan is the most _____ person I know. He has _____ even
with his little brothers. (patience, patient)

3. Mrs. Han likes working in _____. She can _____ any
project she tries. (management, manage)

4. Thomas Edison was a great _____. He liked to _____ new things
in his workshop. (inventor, invent)

5. Sometimes I _____ before making a decision. My _____ means that I am
thinking about it. (hesitate, hesitation)

6. The _____ of the light could be seen for miles. The light had a _____ glow.
(brilliant, brilliance)

7. I take _____ breaks when studying for a test. The _____ of my breaks
decreases as I begin to understand the material better. (frequency, frequent)

8. The radio station's _____ reaches for many miles. The station can

_____ to several different cities. (transmission, transmit)

Writing Skills

Read the story. Then, follow the checklist to use what you learned to write a research paper.

The Tundra

The tundra is a special type of land found in extremely cold areas such as the Arctic and parts of Alaska and Canada. The tundra is sometimes referred to as a frozen desert. In areas with tundra, the ground is frozen the whole year. This permanently frozen ground is called permafrost. Very short shrubs grow in the tundra. It is difficult for taller plants to grow because the ground is so cold and hard. The tundra can be very windy because there is so little to block the wind. Wind speeds can reach nearly 60 miles (about 100 kilometers) per hour. Few animals live in the tundra because there are not many plants. However, many birds and insects travel there in the summertime when the ice on the marshes and lakes melts. Because of the cold, windy conditions, it is difficult for people to live in areas with tundra. Some scientists work on research stations for part of the year to study the plants and animals that live there.

Writing Checklist

_____ 1. Research the tundra using a computer.

_____ 2. Find two websites with credible information. Write them below.

_____

_____

_____ 3. Type a minimum of one page of information about the topic.

_____ 4. Review your work and make revisions with peer editors.

Writing Skills

Read the story. Then, follow the checklist to use what you learned to write a research paper.

The Atmosphere

The atmosphere is the air that surrounds Earth. The air you breathe is part of the atmosphere. Earth's atmosphere contains the gases oxygen, nitrogen, and argon, along with dust, pollen, and water. Oxygen is the most important part of the atmosphere. It is made by plants during their food-making process. In addition to breathing the atmosphere, you can also feel it. When you feel a cool breeze in autumn or warm air on a summer day, you are feeling the atmosphere. The atmosphere has different layers. The troposphere is the layer above the surface of Earth. The troposphere makes up half the atmosphere. All weather occurs in this layer. The next layer is the stratosphere, where jets often fly. This layer absorbs much of the sun's harmful rays. In the mesosphere, the third layer of the atmosphere, rocks from space are caught and burned. The space shuttle orbits in the next layer, the thermosphere. The last layer is the exosphere. After that, you are out in space!

Writing Checklist

_____ 1. Research Earth's atmosphere using your computer.

_____ 2. Find three websites with credible information. Write them below.

_____

_____

_____

_____ 3. Type a minimum of one page of information about the topic.

_____ 4. Review your work and make revisions with peer editors.

Writing Skills

Read the story. Then, follow the checklist to use what you learned to write a research paper.

Climate

The climate describes the weather in an area over a long period of time. If you live somewhere where there are large amounts of yearly rainfall, then you live in a rainy climate. If your town is very hot and dry, then you may live in a desert climate. Some cities, such as San Diego, California, have a very mild climate. Others, such as New Orleans, Louisiana, have warm, heavy air, so they have a humid climate. While the weather in a place may change from day to day, a region's climate seldom changes. Factors other than weather can also affect the climate in a given area. Areas that are close to the sea are cooler and wetter. They may also be cloudy, because clouds form when warm inland air meets the cooler air from the sea. Mountains may also affect climate. Because the temperature at the top of a mountain is cooler than at the ground level, the mountaintop may have year-round snow. Regions near Earth's middle, or equator, are warmer than those at the poles. Sunlight has farther to travel to get to the north and south poles, so these areas are much cooler.

Writing Checklist

_____ 1. Research climate using your computer.

_____ 2. Find four websites with credible information. Write them below.

_____

_____

_____

_____

_____ 3. Type a minimum of one page of information about the topic.

_____ 4. Review your work and make revisions with peer editors.

Writing Skills

Read the story. Then, follow the checklist to use what you learned to write a research paper.

Reading Maps

Have you ever used a map to plan a route? A world map shows the outlines of the continents and seas. It may have parts shaded brown and green to show areas of desert or forest. A city map shows important buildings such as the library or city hall, as well as city streets. Maps use symbols to help you understand them. A compass rose looks like an eight-pointed star inside a circle. It shows you the directions north, south, east, and west. North is usually at the top. A map scale tells you how distances on the map relate to the real world. For example, one inch (2.5 cm) on the map may be equal to 100 miles (160.9 km). A map legend shows you what other symbols mean. A black dot may stand for a city, a star inside a circle may mean a country's capital city, and an airplane may be used to represent an airport. Knowing what these symbols mean makes it much easier to travel.

Writing Checklist

_____   1. Research maps using your computer.

_____   2. Find two websites with credible information. Write them below.

_____

_____

_____   3. Type a minimum of one page of information about the topic.

_____   4. Review your work and make revisions with peer editors.

Writing Skills

Read the story. Then, follow the checklist to use what you learned to write a research paper.

Rainbows

You may have seen a rainbow in the sky after a rainstorm. A rainbow includes the colors red, orange, yellow, green, blue, indigo, and violet. You can remember the order of the colors with the name Roy G. Biv. All of the colors combined create white light. A rainbow is formed when a ray of sunlight shines through a cloud, refracts off the water droplets, and is split into bands of color. Rainbows are fairly rare to see. This is because special conditions are required for them to become visible. To see a rainbow, you must have rain in front of you, at a distance, and the sun behind you, low on the horizon. The curve of the rainbow is in the direction opposite from the sun. Rainbows are more common in summertime, because you must have both rain and warm sunlight to see them. Because there is less sunlight and more frozen water, rainbows are less likely to form during winter.

Writing Checklist

_____ 1. Research rainbows using your computer.

_____ 2. Find three websites with credible information. Write them below.

_____

_____

_____

_____ 3. Type a minimum of one page of information about the topic.

_____ 4. Review your work and make revisions with peer editors.

Writing Skills

Read the story. Then, follow the checklist to use what you learned to write a research paper.

Salmon

Animals such as dogs and cats may spend their entire lives in the same city or town in which they were born. Other animals, however, travel great distances during their life cycle. The salmon swims from the rivers of Alaska to the Pacific Ocean and back again. The salmon lays its eggs in the riverbed. After about three months, the eggs hatch. Then, the tiny fish swim around the rivers until they are large enough to travel to the sea. As the fish grow older and larger, they develop patterns that look like finger marks along their sides. Once they are one to three years old, they move in groups toward the ocean. Their bodies change so they can live in salt water instead of freshwater. The young salmon then spend several years swimming in the ocean. Eventually, they will swim back to the river in which they were born. There they lay eggs, and the cycle begins again.

Writing Checklist

_____ 1. Research salmon using your computer.

_____ 2. Find four websites with credible information. Write them below.

_____

_____

_____

_____

_____ 3. Type a minimum of one page of information about the topic.

_____ 4. Review your work and make revisions with peer editors.

Nouns

A **noun** is a word that names a person, place, or thing.

Read the story below. Some of the nouns are missing. Fill in the blanks with the words from the word box below.

apartment	brother	students	art	family
library	place	state	teacher	notice
school	work	mother	club	projects

Raven and her little _____ needed a new _____ to go after school. They

usually went to their aunt's _____, but she was moving to another _____.

Raven's _____ did not finish _____ early enough to pick them up at school.

Raven saw a _____ at _____ about a new _____ that was

forming. It was for _____ aged eight to ten. They would meet after school, walk to the

_____ with the art _____, and work on art _____ until

someone from their _____ could come get them. Raven thought that was perfect! She loved

_____, and so did her brother. She could not wait to tell Mom.

Nouns

Read the story below. Some of the nouns are missing. Fill in the blanks with the words from the word box below.

topic	something	class	model	magnets
salad	science	planets	system	friends
advice	stepdad	project	plants	garden
ideas	tomatoes			

Stefani needed to choose a creative _____ for science _____. First, she

wanted to study _____. She could show how to pull them apart. Then, she thought she

would build a _____ of the solar _____. She could show how the different

_____ moved. Finally, Stefani thought about growing tomato _____. She

liked working in the _____. Stefani had many good _____. She asked her

_____ which _____ to choose. He said, "Pick _____ that

the whole family will enjoy." Stefani thought that was great _____. She decided to grow

_____. She could make a tasty _____ when she was done! Her project for

_____ was delicious. She wanted to share it with her _____.

Nouns

Read the story below. Some of the nouns are missing. Fill in the blanks with the words from the word box below.

mother	suit	hills	weekend	dad
neighborhood	park	socks	pavement	store
hobby	morning	lunchtime	block	shoes
family	treadmill	sister		

Lakshmi's _____ loved to run. He ran down the streets in their _____

every _____ before sunrise. Then, he ran once around the _____

at _____. He also ran up and down the steep _____ by the city

_____ each _____ morning. Lakshmi thought this _____

looked like fun. She asked her dad if she could run with him. Dad said, "Sure!" He took Lakshmi to the

_____ to buy a track _____ and _____ that would keep her

feet dry. Finally, they bought running _____. Now Lakshmi's older _____

wants to run too! Soon, her whole _____ will be running. Her _____

wanted to give it a try. She practiced on the _____ on the weekend. She is ready to hit the

_____!

Verbs

A **verb** is a word that tells what kind of action is being performed.

Read the story below. Some of the verbs are missing. Fill in the blanks with the words from the word box below.

fry	like	picks	tastes	stop
arrive	buy	helps	wait	take
have	wake	brings	puts	cast

Benny and his sister Hannah _____ to go fishing with their uncle. They

_____ up early on a Saturday morning. Uncle Ray _____ them up in his

old pickup truck. He _____ fishing rods and an icebox. They _____ to

_____ bait and cold drinks on the way to the lake. When they _____,

Uncle Ray _____ the bait on the hook. He _____ Benny and

Hannah _____ their lines into the water. Then, they _____ for a fish

to _____ the bait. Soon they _____ enough fish for dinner. They

_____ the fish with vegetables. It _____ great!

Verbs

Read the story below. Some of the verbs are missing. Fill in the blanks with the words from the word box below.

laugh	watch	showed	dressed	sounded
went	were	felt	looked	smiled
felt	loved	called	knew	was
play	cheered			

Keesha _____ to _____ her older sister, Kendra, _____

volleyball. She _____ in the colors for Kendra's school and _____ to all of

the games. She _____ until she _____ hoarse. Kendra _____

Keesha her biggest fan. Keesha _____ sad that she _____ too small to play

volleyball. Kendra and the rest of her teammates _____ very tall. One day Keesha's mom

_____ her a picture of Kendra when she was Keesha's age. Kendra _____

just like Keesha did now. Keesha _____ and started to _____. "Kendra was

small once too! Maybe I can play volleyball one day after all." Keesha _____ proud of

herself. She _____ she could do it!

Verbs

Read the story below. Some of the verbs are missing. Fill in the blanks with the words from the word box below.

gets	walk	has	walked	loves
started	turned	exercise	stepped	would
does	walks	trusts	works	opened
called	come	running		

Kamran _____ a new after-school job. His neighbor, Mr. Quigley, just

_____ coaching soccer in the evenings, and he _____ not have time

to _____ home after work. Mr. Quigley said he _____ Kamran to

_____ his dog, Leo. Kamran _____ Leo to the park and back before he

_____ on his homework. On the first day of Kamran's new job, he _____

the gate and _____ Leo's name. Leo came _____. He was ready

for his walk! As Kamran and Leo _____ down the street, another neighbor, Mrs.

Pellini, _____ out of her house. She asked, "Kamran, _____ you

_____ my dog too? Katie _____ to go to the park." Now Kamran

_____ twice the exercise! His after-school job _____ into a business and

a workout routine.

Adjectives

An **adjective** is a word that describes something.

Read the story below. Some of the adjectives are missing. Fill in the blanks with the words from the word box below.

enormous	beautiful	dark	quiet	awful
better	great	inspiring	fine	sad
nervous	cheerful	deep	bright	shaky

My choir director, Mrs. Rosas, is an _____ person. She helps us memorize

_____ songs so that we can give a _____ performance. When I tried out for

the choir, I was very _____. My voice was _____ and _____,

and I thought that I sounded _____. Mrs. Rosas smiled and said she knew that I could

do a _____ job. She told me to take a _____ breath and try the song

again. This time I sounded _____! Our choir wears _____ red shirts with

_____ pants when we sing. Being in the choir makes me feel _____. If I am

_____ when I start singing, by the end of the song I have an _____ smile on

my face again.

Adjectives

Read the story below. Some of the adjectives are missing. Fill in the blanks with the words from the word box below.

marvelous	wonderful	older	fun	favorite
lengthy	yellow	giant	surprised	nice
closest	fabulous	special	front	long
happy	blue			

Leticia and her _____ brother, Amos, wanted to plan a _____

surprise party for their mom. She always threw parties for them that were _____

and _____. Now it would be her own _____ day. Leticia made

a _____ list of all of her mom's _____ friends. Mom was such a

_____ person, everyone wanted to be her friend. Amos ordered a _____

cake with _____ and _____ icing to feed all of the guests. These were Mom's

_____ colors. On the day of the party, Leticia asked Mom to go on a _____

walk. When they got home, all of Mom's friends were hiding in the living room. When Mom opened the

_____ door, they all shouted, "Surprise!" Mom said it was the most _____

party ever. She felt _____ and very _____.

Adjectives

Read the story below. Some of the adjectives are missing. Fill in the blanks with the words from the word box below.

famous	long	vast	slender	longer
brilliant	creative	green	deep	enormous
dark	tiny	best	whole	great
detailed	proud	exciting		

Angelica decided to write a book. She loved to read, and her teachers said that she had

a _____ imagination. Her heroine would have _____ eyes and

_____, _____ hair, just like Angelica. She would live in the middle of a

_____, _____ forest. Angelica imagined the animals that might come to

visit her character— _____ bears, _____ deer, and _____

mice. She worked on her _____ story every day at lunchtime and after school. It

grew _____ and soon took up a _____ notebook! Angelica let her

_____ friend, Mindy, read her story. Mindy thought it was _____ and very

_____. She said she could not wait until Angelica was a _____ author one

day! Mindy felt _____ of her friend. She loved reading Angelica's _____

stories.

Homophones

> **Homophones** are words that sound alike but are spelled differently and have different meanings.

Write the correct homophone on the line.

1. _____, you may not have any candy before dinner.

2. I don't _____ what street Julio lives on.

3. There are _____ dogs allowed here.

> **no:** antonym of yes
>
> **know:** verb, to understand

4. Julian has a _____ bike.

5. Willow _____ where Paco lived.

6. The _____ theater has comfortable seats.

> **new:** not old
>
> **knew:** verb, past tense of know

7. Put your name in the upper _____ corner.

8. Please _____ your name on the paper.

9. Yes, that answer is _____.

> **write:** verb, to make purposeful marks, for example with a pencil
>
> **right:** to be correct or a direction opposite of left

10. We are not _____ to chew gum in school.

11. When you read _____, it bothers me.

12. Are we _____ to bring pets to school?

> **allowed:** permitted
>
> **aloud:** out loud

Homophones

After each sentence below are two homophones. Write the homophone that makes sense in the sentence on the line. Write a sentence using the other homophone on the line.

1. The _____ of the tree hung low over the sidewalk. (bough, bow)

   _____

2. Jane had been sick for over a week and was _____ staying in bed. (board, bored)

   _____

3. The wranglers watched the _____ on the range. (heard, herd)

   _____

4. Dick and Tom passed _____ the passage that led into the cave. (threw, through)

   _____

5. An _____ is a type of boat. (ark, arc)

   _____

6. In _____ shop did you find your new shoes? (witch, which)

   _____

7. Father stopped and asked the _____ to the stadium. (way, weigh)

   _____

8. The campers put a _____ over the fire and put water on it to boil. (great, grate)

   _____

Homophones

Read each sentence and choose the set of homophones from the list below that belongs. Write the correct homophone on each line. Not all the homophone sets will be used.

capital	threw	heal	grays	principle	patience
capitol	through	heel	graze	principal	patients
chute	cord	heir	I'll	whey	rein
shoot	chord	air	isle	weigh	reign
			aisle	way	rain

1. The cows did _____ under clouds of different colored _____.

2. _____ walk down the tree-covered _____ on the

   tropical _____.

3. I want to _____ your picture when you race down the water _____.

4. When the pianist hit the song's first _____, an electrical _____ shorted
   and the concert hall went dark.

5. The doctor's _____ had little _____ when they learned the doctor would
   be an hour late.

6. We drove to our state's _____, Springfield, Illinois, and we got a tour

   of the _____.

7. Tim _____ a ball _____ the air for his dog to chase.

8. The prince would someday be _____ to the throne, and he promised to clean up

   the polluted _____.

9. The one _____ that the _____ expected the students to maintain was
   "always do your very best, and you will feel success."

10. John had a sore on his _____ that would not _____.

Answer Key

Name _____   4.RL.1, 4.RL.3, 4.RL.10

Character Analysis

Read the story. Then, answer the questions.

Neighbors Need Neighbors

There was an old lady who lived on the edge of town. Everyone referred to her as Granny. Because she kept to herself, she seemed a little different to some. She asked nothing of anyone and did nothing for anyone, except her many dogs. The number of dogs varied daily. Some only came when they were hungry and then left until they returned to eat again. Some knew a good home and stayed.

One day the paper boy noticed Granny's papers had not been picked up for three or four days. The dogs in her yard were thin and moved about slowly. He had not seen Granny for about a week. He wondered if she was all right.

He got off his bike and walked up the steps onto the front porch. He walked around and peered in the windows, but he did not see anything. He opened the front door slightly and called, "Hello! Anyone here?" He listened for a minute. He thought he heard a whimpering sound, so he quickly rode to the closest neighbor's house and called 9-1-1.

When the police arrived they found Granny had fallen and had not been able to move to call for help. The paramedics said Granny needed to go to the hospital where she stayed a few days.

While she was in the hospital, the paper boy came to feed her dogs every day. When Granny came home, neighbors brought food and flowers. Granny was sorry she had not gotten to know her new friends sooner, but was glad she had now "found" them.

1. Circle what Granny's behavior said about her character at the beginning of the story.

   (She liked to be alone.)   She did not like people.   She was mean.

2. How did Granny's behavior change?

   She kept to herself and seemed a little different to some.

3. How did the neighbors' feelings for Granny change?

   The neighbors brought food and flowers, and showed they cared for Granny.

Name _____   4.RL.1, 4.RL.3, 4.RL.10

Character Analysis

Read the story. Then, answer the questions.

The Grass Is Always Greener

Once upon a time there was a princess named Priscilla. She had a normal infancy, but when she began to walk her life changed. She was not allowed to go anywhere without being chaperoned by at least five of the royal guards. She wanted to play with other children her age, but her parents did not want her outside the castle walls.

One day she managed to escape the guards' watchful eyes. She ran off to the forest. When she stopped running, she found herself amidst towering trees with hardly any sunlight filtering through their leafy branches. Squirrels ran from tree to tree, a deer sailed by, and from the treetops she heard unusual bird songs she had never heard before.

Suddenly an ugly creature popped out from the shrubbery. He introduced himself as Whiz. He was a wizard and could grant her one wish. Priscilla did not hesitate. She knew just what she wanted. "Oh please, I would like to play with some children outside the castle's walls."

"Not a problem," said Whiz. Immediately she was on a playground in the middle of a dodgeball game. Because she did not know the rules, she was hit with the ball and out of the game. That was not fun. The next game was tag, but she did not know to run so she was always caught. She was therefore always "it." She was exhausted. She was not sure playing with other children was fun. She began to want to go home but did not know exactly where it was.

Luckily the guards who were looking for her came by. When she saw them she jumped for joy. She jumped so high that she landed on the back of a guard's horse and rode home in record time.

Circle how Priscilla felt in each situation.

1. When guards were watching her: angry   (unhappy)   contented

2. When she was lost in woods: (frightened)   entranced   free

3. When she got her wish: let down   (elated)   scared

4. Playing dodgeball and tag: hurt   playful   (discouraged)

5. When she saw the guards: (relieved)   resentful   encouraged

---

Name _____   4.RL.1, 4.RL.3, 4.RL.10

Character Analysis

Read each paragraph and answer the questions.

Robbie and his dad were walking on the beach on a summer morning. They were talking about how beautiful the beach was. They were looking for signs of animals while the tide was low. Robbie saw something large up ahead on the beach. He and his dad ran toward it. It was a giant whale beached on the sand. Robbie's dad quickly ran to the nearest house so he could call the aquarium.

1. a. Who are the main characters in the story? **Robbie and his dad**

   b. What is the setting? **The setting is the beach on a summer morning.**

   c. What is the problem? **There was a giant beached whale on the sand.**

   d. How do you think the story will end? **Answers will vary.**

Marjie brought her new bike to Danielle's house. Danielle and Marjie took turns riding the new bike. They each rode it around the block several times. Marjie showed Danielle how she could ride her bike without holding the handlebars. Danielle wanted to try, too. Danielle got started and shouted, "Look, no hands!" Then Danielle fell on the sidewalk. She got up right away. Marjie asked if she was all right. Danielle said, "I'm fine, but I think your handlebars are twisted."

2. a. Who are the main characters in the story? **Marjie and Danielle**

   b. What is the setting? **Danielle's house and the block are the settings.**

   c. What is the problem? **Danielle fell on the sidewalk.**

   d. How do you think the story will end? **Answers will vary.**

Name _____   4.RL.6, 4.RL.10

Point of View

Point of view refers to the person who is telling the story or "speaking." When you write a letter, you are writing in "first person," which includes the words I, me, my, we, and our. Second-person writing occurs when the author talks about you and yours, and third person includes the words he, she, they, his, her, and their. In third-person writing, the author does not put himself in the story.

A story can be told from different points of view.

In **first person**, the main character tells the story.

In **second person**, the story is told as though it is happening to you.

In **third person**, a narrator tells the story as if she is watching it happen.

Read each story and circle the point of view.

1. Marcus's family had just moved to a large city from a very small town. He was surprised at how many cars were on the street and how few people said hello when he met them on the sidewalk. In his old town, he had known everyone. He hoped that he would make a new friend on the first day of school. When he saw the crowded hallways as he walked into the building, he felt worried. Then, he thought to himself that with all those people around, he was sure to make a lot of friends.

   first person   second person   (third person)

2. When my family moved to the big city, I was excited about all of the new activities we could try. I never thought about how crowded it might be. Back home, my neighbors were very friendly. It seemed like I knew everyone in the whole town. I wanted to make new friends in the city, but when I got to school the hallways were so packed I could hardly get to my classroom. I took a deep breath and thought to myself, "With all of these people around, I am sure to make new friends."

   (first person)   second person   third person

Answer Key

Name _____ 4.RL.6, 4.RL.10

Point of View

> Remember, a story can be told from different points of view.
>> In **first person**, the main character tells the story.
>> In **second person**, the story is told as though it is happening to you.
>> In **third person**, a narrator tells the story as if she is watching it happen.

Read each story and circle the point of view.

1. I love gardening. Seeing the little sprouts push up through the ground in early spring makes my heart sing. It can be hard to wait until the plants are fully grown to eat them. My brother likes vegetables, and he enjoys tomatoes in particular. Every year he tries to harvest them too early. At the end of the summer, I gather seeds and plant my crop for the next year. It is fun to see the whole growing cycle.

   (first person)   second person   third person

2. You love to work in the garden. You especially like seeing the tiny plants first appear through the dirt. Although it is hard to wait, you know that it is better to wait until the plants are fully grown before pulling them up. Your brother is so fond of tomatoes that his mouth begins to water even before they are red. At summer's end, you gather seeds to plant for next spring. You rejoice at the cycle of nature.

   first person   (second person)   third person

3. Carrie often worked in her garden. She checked the soil every morning to see if any new plants had appeared. Sometimes her brother tried to pick a green tomato, but she always stopped him. She said that it was better to wait until they were ripe. When the summer was over, she planted seeds for a new crop.

   first person   second person   (third person)

Name _____ 4.RL.6, 4.RL.10

Point of View

Read each story and circle the point of view.

1. Felipe loved to cook. He had been helping his mom and grandma in the kitchen ever since he could remember. One day Mom suggested he cook dinner for Grandma. Felipe was nervous but excited. He wrote a grocery list and asked Mom to take him shopping. They chose fresh vegetables and herbs for a delicious stew. Felipe had watched Grandma cook the stew many times. He thought he could cook it perfectly even without a recipe, as long as Mom was there to answer any questions.

   first person   second person   (third person)

2. I love to cook. I first started helping my mom and grandma in the kitchen when I was very small. One day Mom suggested I cook dinner for Grandma. I felt excited but also a little nervous. I had never cooked a meal by myself before! Mom and I went to the store with a list of food to buy. She showed me how to choose fresh vegetables and special herbs. I have watched Grandma make stew many times, so I think that I can cook it even without a list of instructions. Mom will be standing by to help just in case.

   (first person)   second person   third person

3. Your favorite activity is cooking. You have been helping your family in the kitchen since you were a child. One day your mom suggests you cook dinner for Grandma. You are excited but nervous, since you have never cooked a whole dinner by yourself before. You help your mom make a list of things to buy, and then you go to the store. You pick out only the freshest vegetables. Because you have watched Grandma make her special stew many times before, you know you can make it without using a recipe and with only a little help from Mom.

   first person   (second person)   third person

4. You and your family have just moved to the city. You are surprised at seeing so many cars on the road. In your old town, you felt like you knew everyone. When you drive up to the school, your mother wishes you good luck. You walk into the building and start to look for your classroom. You think that with all these people around, you are sure to make some new friends.

   first person   (second person)   third person

Name _____ 4.RL.6, 4.RL.10

Point of View

> Point of view refers to the person who is telling the story or "speaking." When you write a letter, you are writing in "first person," which includes the words *I, me, my, we,* and *our.* Second-person writing occurs when the author talks about you and yours, and third person includes the words *he, she, they, his, her,* and *their.* In third-person writing, the author does not put himself in the story.
>
> A story can be told from different points of view.
>> In **first person**, the main character tells the story.
>> In **second person**, the story is told as though it is happening to you.
>> In **third person**, a narrator tells the story as if she is watching it happen.

Read each story and circle the point of view.

1. You have been looking forward to the big class picnic for a long time. You and your friends hope to look for wildflowers after you eat lunch. You want to find 10 different kinds of flowers. When the day of the picnic comes, it starts to rain. You are sad at first, but then your teacher reminds you that the flowers need rain to grow. You smile to yourself and think that next time you can try to find 20 different wildflowers.

   first person   (second person)   third person

2. I had been looking forward to the class picnic for weeks. My friends and I were planning to pick wildflowers after eating our sandwiches. I hoped I could find 10 different kinds of flowers! On the day of the picnic, it was raining. I felt sad at first, but I knew that the rain would help the flowers grow even bigger. The next time we went on a picnic, maybe I could find 20 kinds of flowers!

   (first person)   second person   third person

Name _____ 4.RL.6, 4.RL.10

Point of View

> Remember, a story can be told from different points of view.
>> In **first person**, the main character tells the story.
>> In **second person**, the story is told as though it is happening to you.
>> In **third person**, a narrator tells the story as if she is watching it happen.

Read each story and circle the point of view.

1. Clara ran home from school and checked the mailbox. She was disappointed to find that the mail had not come yet. She was expecting a letter from a special friend. Clara had a pen pal in Korea named Chi. They sometimes sent e-mail to each other, but both girls liked getting letters and funny postcards. Just then there was a knock at the door. It was the postman! He smiled and handed Clara a letter with a Korean postmark.

   first person   second person   (third person)

2. I ran home from school yesterday and checked the mailbox. My letter from Chi was not there yet! Chi is my pen pal. She lives in Korea. We sometimes send e-mail to each other, but we both like getting postcards with funny pictures too. I was getting a snack when I heard a knock at the door. It was the mailman, and he had a letter for me! He smiled and said, "Tell Chi I said hello."

   (first person)   second person   third person

3. You run home from school to check the mailbox. You are disappointed when the letter you are expecting is not there. You are hoping for a letter from your pen pal, Chi, who lives in Korea. You like to send e-mail to each other, but you also like getting postcards and letters in the mail. You hear a knock at the door. It is the mailman, and he has a letter from Chi.

   first person   (second person)   third person

Answer Key

Name _____ (4.RL.6, 4.RL.10)

Point of View
Read each story and circle the point of view.

1. I like rain, and I like sun, but I like snow most of all. Winter is a fun season. I like building snowmen with my brothers and making a fort with snowballs. I like lying in the snow and making patterns with my arms. I help Dad shovel snow off the pathways so that people can walk and drive safely. I also help Mom make cocoa and cookies to warm us up when we come back indoors.

    (first person)   second person   third person

2. Lupe liked all kinds of weather, but she liked snow most of all. Winter was her favorite season. She liked to build snowmen with her brothers. Sometimes they made a fort with snowballs. Lupe liked to lie in the snow and make patterns with her arms. She helped her dad shovel the sidewalks so that people could walk safely. She also helped her mom make cocoa and bake cookies to warm everyone up when they came back indoors.

    first person   second person   (third person)

3. You like rain and sun, but you like the snow in winter most of all. You like to build snowmen with your brothers and make forts with snowballs. You like to lie in the snow and make patterns with your arms. You help your father move snow off the sidewalks. Then, you help your mom make cocoa and cookies to warm everyone up!

    first person   (second person)   third person

4. Dreama and her friends had been looking forward to the class picnic all month long. They wanted to eat sandwiches in the field and then pick beautiful wildflowers. Dreama was hoping to find 10 different kinds of flowers. When she woke up on the day of the picnic, it was raining. Dreama felt sad at first, but she knew that the flowers needed rain to grow. Maybe at the next picnic she could find even more kinds of flowers.

    first person   second person   (third person)

13

Name _____ (4.RL.2, 4.RL.10)

Theme
Read each paragraph below. Then, circle the theme of the story.

The Hare and the Tortoise
One day a hare was making fun of a tortoise and called him a slowpoke. That made the tortoise mad, so he challenged the hare to a race. Of course, the hare knew he would win. When the hare got far enough ahead, he stopped for a rest and fell asleep. The tortoise plodded along, never stopping. When the hare woke up, he ran as fast as he could to the finish line. However, the tortoise had already crossed it. The moral of the story is . . .

1. a. A lazy hare is fast.
   (b.) Do not brag.
   c. The slow turtle wins.

The Fox and the Crow
A crow sat in a tree with a piece of cheese it had just taken from an open window. A fox who was walking by saw the crow and wanted the cheese. The fox complimented the crow in many ways. One was to tell the crow how nicely it sang. To prove its voice, the crow opened up his mouth to sing. The cheese fell out, and the fox gobbled it up. The moral of the story is . . .

2. (a.) Do not let flattery go to your head.
   b. Listen before you sing.
   c. Eat fast so you will not lose your dinner.

The Dog and the Bone
A dog was walking over a bridge carrying a bone. The dog looked into the stream and saw another dog carrying a bigger bone. The dog on the bridge jumped into the water because he wanted the bigger bone. But he dropped his, and there was no other bone. The moral of the story is . . .

3. a. He lost his bone.
   b. The dog was wet.
   (c.) Think before you act.

14

Name _____ (4.RL.2, 4.RL.10)

Theme
Read the paragraphs below. Then, write the theme of each story.

Because Tammy had to stay after school, she had to ride her bicycle home in the dark. The ride was scary because there were no lights on the dirt road that led to her house. Finally, she could see the lights of her house in the distance, so she pedaled faster. She was not paying close attention to the road when she hit something. Her bike went flying one way and she another. Tammy landed in a soft pile of hay. When she realized she was all right, she climbed up onto the road. Lying in the middle of the road was a box that had broken apart when she hit it. Inside she could see money. She ran the rest of the way home to tell her family what had happened and to make a sign to find the owner of the box.

1. **Answers will vary but may include don't be afraid of the** **unknown.**

It was snowing hard, and Justin was taking a freshly baked apple pie to Mrs. Harper's house for his mother. Mrs. Harper lived only two blocks from Justin's, but because of the fast falling snow it was difficult for Justin to see any pathways. He trudged on, and snow began to accumulate in large drifts. After a while, Justin did not see anything familiar—just white falling from the sky and white on the ground. He did not know which way to go. He was lost. What seemed like hours passed. Finally, he saw some lights and heard a loud scratching sound. It came closer and got louder. It was a snowplow. The driver asked if he was Justin. Justin was relieved and hopped into the truck's cab. Justin had gone the opposite way of Mrs. Harper's house. When he had not arrived in what should have been a few minutes, she called the city who sent someone out looking for him. Mrs. Harper got her pie, and Justin got a ride home.

2. **Answers will vary but may include weather can be** **dangerous.**

15

Name _____ (4.RL.2, 4.RL.10)

Theme
Read the story.

Shortcut
We probably should have taken the road home from the baseball park. It was getting dark, though, and we decided to take the shortcut home. I was the oldest and should have made a better choice. I didn't know there would be a train.

The shortcut from the baseball park to home was along the train tracks. After Reggie's game was over, we were excited. The game had gone into extra innings and Reggie's team had won! As we walked, Reggie and I gave each other high fives. Samantha and little Brittany were running to keep up. You know how little sisters are. When we came to the turn for the shortcut, we were so excited and happy that we just took it. We should have stayed on the road.

We walked for about five minutes on the tracks. The sides of the tracks were steep and there were thick bushes and marshy water at the bottom. We stayed on the tracks. Samantha asked how we'd know if a train was coming. I said that we'd feel the tracks rumbling.

It was then that I heard the train whistle far away. I didn't want to worry the little ones, so I just said as calmly as I could, "Let's go back to the road." We turned around and I walked pretty fast. Everyone followed.

Soon we felt the tracks rumbling and I shouted, "Run!" I grabbed little Brittany in my arms and Reggie held Samantha's hand. We ran as fast as we could. Then I could see the headlights and the train blew its loud whistle. We kept running, but I shouted, "Get off the track, NOW!" We jumped off the tracks and slid down the sides. Samantha and Brittany were crying but I could not hear them. The loud train was rushing by us.

After the train went by, we climbed back up the hill. We were all scratched up from the bushes, but no one complained. We were all shaking as we walked back to the road. We didn't have to talk. We all knew we'd never take the shortcut home again.

Choose a theme for the story. Then, give several reasons to explain why you chose this theme.

Answers will vary but may include consider your choices **carefully.**

_____

_____

_____

_____

16

Answer Key

Name _____

(4.RL.1, 4.RL.7, 4.RL.10)

Referring to Details

Read the story.

Peterson's Pockets

I love pockets! When I pick out a new coat each year, I look for the coat with the most pockets. I especially like hidden pockets. I once had a coat with 12 pockets! I loved that coat.

I also love pants with lots of pockets. I love those pants that have pockets on the side of the leg. I like to put things in my pockets. I put money, bottle caps, cool stones, my yo-yo, notes from my friends, and other stuff I find in my pockets.

My mom doesn't like it that I put stuff in my pockets. Sometimes I forget to take papers out of my pockets before my mom washes my pants. She says it makes an awful mess in the washing machine.

My dad said that long, long ago, pants didn't have any pockets at all! Back then, people wore little pouches that hung from their belts. I would have had to wear a pretty big pouch. My mom says I would have to carry around a suitcase if I didn't have all these pockets.

Did you know that the first pockets on pants were little pouches sewn on the outside of the pants? About 200 years ago, pockets finally were sewn on the inside of pants like they are now.

Someday, I'm going to invent a new place to hide a pocket. Maybe in 200 years, people will be talking about me and my super cool pocket. They will wonder how people ever got along without the "Peterson pocket."

Think of a new place to hide a pocket. Then draw a design to enhance the story. Use labels to describe where the pocket is and what it could hold. Underline the parts of the story that helped you design the pocket.

> **Drawings will vary.**
>
> **Check students' underlining.**

Name _____

(4.RL.1, 4.RL.4, 4.RL.10)

Referring to Details

Read the story. Then, answer the questions. Underline the parts of the story that helped you answer each question.

Penny's New Glasses

Penny had a hard time seeing the board in class. Rosa sat next to her. Penny asked Rosa to read her the assignment each day. One day, their teacher said, "Penny, I think you should go to the eye doctor."

Penny's mom made an appointment, and, in a few weeks, Penny was waiting in the office of the optometrist. The optometrist called her name and she went into a darkened room. On one side of the room was a large chair with a robot-looking machine in front of it. The doctor told her to sit in the chair. The doctor sat on a small stool on rollers and introduced herself. "I'm Dr. Riley."

Dr. Riley pulled the machine over to Penny. Part of the machine looked like a mask. Dr. Riley told Penny to look through the mask and read some letters on the opposite wall. As Dr. Riley turned some dials, the letters became blurry and then clear. Dr. Riley kept turning dials until Penny said that the letters were very clear and easy to read.

Penny picked out small, round frames that were black. The optician told Penny that her glasses would be ready in about a week. Penny wished she could wear her new glasses home. She was excited.

In a week, Penny went back and picked up her new glasses. She liked the way she looked with her glasses. Her mom said she looked smart.

The next day at school, Penny wore her new glasses. She couldn't wait to show her friends. "It's about time you got glasses," Rosa said. "I'm tired of reading the board for you." Penny laughed when Rosa smiled.

During math, Penny could read the problems on the board. In reading, she had no trouble reading her book. In gym class, Penny made a basket. She felt great about how clear everything was now.

Check students' underlining.

1. Why did Penny's teacher think Penny should go to the eye doctor?

   Penny's teacher noticed Penny had a hard time seeing in class.

2. How did the eye doctor know how strong Penny's glasses should be?

   The eye doctor knew because she used a special machine.

3. What does an optometrist do?

   An optometrist can prescribe glasses to people with trouble seeing.

Name _____

(4.RL.1, 4.RL.10, 4.RF.4)

Referring to Details

Read the story.

Lemonade Stand

Faiza and Emily set up a small wooden table at the corner of Cambridge and Sherman Streets. Faiza set up the supplies. Emily set up two chairs and a large umbrella. Soon they would be open for business.

The girls painted a sign. They lettered the sign carefully: "Lemonade for Sale." They leaned the sign in front of the table.

Then the girls went inside and came back with a heavy cooler. Inside were two pitchers of lemonade and a bag of ice. They also had homemade cookies.

They took one pitcher and set it on the table. Then they put 10 cookies on a plate. They sat down in their chairs and waited.

A car drove by. It didn't stop. A few minutes later, another car drove past. Emily yelled, "Lemonade for sale!" The car kept driving. A third car came by and parked at the neighbor's house. Faiza and Emily both shouted, "Lemonade for sale! Twenty-five cents a cup!" Faiza's neighbor stepped out of the car. She walked over to the lemonade stand.

"Hi, Mrs. Ford," said Emily. "Would you like some lemonade?"

"Sure," said Mrs. Ford. She gave the girls a quarter and drank her cold lemonade. She also bought two cookies and said good-bye.

Emily and Faiza stayed at their lemonade stand for two hours. Many people bought lemonade and cookies. By the time they ran out of lemonade and cookies, they had earned six dollars.

Underline each event in the story. Then, put the events of the day in order by numbering the sentences from 1 to 10.

__4__ They carried out the heavy cooler.

__2__ Emily set up the chairs.

__8__ The neighbor bought some lemonade.

__1__ The girls set up the table.

__6__ They put 10 cookies on a plate.

__5__ They put one pitcher of lemonade on the table.

__9__ The girls stayed at the lemonade stand for two hours.

__10__ They earned six dollars.

__3__ They painted the sign.

__7__ Two cars drove by without stopping.

Name _____

(4.RL.1, 4.RL.7, 4.RL.10)

Referring to Details

Read the recipe. Then, follow the directions.

Campfire Walking Salad

Before you pick up your hot dog at the campfire, make a walking salad. You won't need a fork or plate for this salad. Just wrap the salad fixings in a piece of lettuce and carry it in one hand.

Ingredients:

large lettuce leaves   mayonnaise
salted Spanish peanuts   peanut butter
miniature marshmallows   raisins
raw carrot shavings

Directions:

Wash and pat dry several leaves of Bibb or leaf lettuce. Set out the ingredients on a table. Choose a lettuce leaf and spread mayonnaise or peanut butter on it. Then add other toppings. Roll up the lettuce like a tortilla and eat.

Draw the steps for making a walking salad. Label the steps and the ingredients. Underline the parts of the recipe that helped you draw each step.

Check students' drawings.	
1.	2.
3.	4.

Answer Key

Name

4.RL.1, 4.RL.3, 4.RL.10

Referring to Details

Read the story. Then, answer the questions. Underline the parts of the story that helped you answer each question.

A Day at the Beach

Erika and Yesenia rode together in the backseat. They were excited because they were going to the beach. Erika had never been to the beach before. She was going with her best friend Yesenia's family.

Yesenia told Erika all about the sand and the waves. She told her about the paddle boat. "I like to paddle out to the deep part and jump in the water," said Yesenia. Erika felt her stomach tighten. She didn't know how to swim. She didn't know that Yesenia was so brave in the water.

The girls had a great time. They played in the water, jumping in the waves and laughing. They built a huge sand castle using buckets and shovels. Erika thought the beach was great!

Then Yesenia's dad called them over to the boat dock. He had the paddle boat ready for them and held two life jackets in his hands. Yesenia ran to the boat, put on her life jacket, and sat down. She smiled and waited for Erika. Erika was very nervous. Yesenia's dad helped her put on her life jacket. Yesenia started pedaling so Erika did too. They were moving quickly across the water. When they were far out in the lake, Yesenia stopped the boat and said, "Last one in the lake has stinky feet!" Yesenia jumped in the water. Erika didn't move. She didn't dare tell Yesenia that she couldn't swim. Would Yesenia laugh at her?

Yesenia watched Erika. Finally she said, "Are you coming in?" When Erika shrugged her shoulders, Yesenia guessed what was wrong. "Do you know how to swim yet?" she asked kindly. Erika shook her head. Yesenia smiled at her friend and said, "Okay. Let's paddle around some more. Then after lunch, I'll teach you a little bit about swimming." Erika smiled at her best friend. Why had she ever worried about telling Yesenia that she didn't know how to swim?

Answers will vary but may include:

1. What do you think Yesenia would have done if Erika had told her right away that she couldn't swim?

She would have been kind and understanding.

2. Why do you think Erika waited to tell Yesenia that she couldn't swim?

Erika felt shy, ashamed, or embarrassed because she could

not swim.

3. Why do you think Erika didn't know how to swim?

Erika did not learn as a child.

4. What did the girls have fun doing at the beach?

They played in the water or built a sand castle.

Name

4.RL.1, 4.RL.3, 4.RL.10

Referring to Details

Read the story. Then, answer the questions. Underline the parts of the story that helped you answer each question.

A Family Hike

We started on the trail early in the morning. The sun was rising in the sky and the air around us was cold and misty. The pine trees looked like arrows pointing our way to the top of the mountain.

My mom and dad each carried a heavy backpack full of food, tents, water, and other things. Ben and I carried packs, too. Mine only had my clothes and sleeping bag in it. I carried a few snacks in my pockets and two water bottles on my belt. Ben carried some food and a cookstove in his pack.

We walked quietly at first. My dad says you don't need words to be part of the forest in the morning. I could hear birds singing and chipmunks moving through the leaves on the ground. There was no breeze so the trees were silent. We walked single file along the trail.

At lunchtime, we stopped by a stream that flowed down the mountain. We could see a small waterfall higher up, but here the water cut through the rock and snaked past flowers and bushes. We took off our shoes and dipped our feet in the water. The sun shone brightly overhead and we all took off our jackets.

I knew better than to ask how much farther we had to go. We would be walking for three days on these trails. We would see many beautiful sights and hear and smell things we don't hear or smell at home in the city. My mom and dad are teachers. Every summer, we take a trip as a family.

We went to bed pretty early because we were all tired from walking. Tomorrow, we will have another long walk. We will reach the top of the mountain tomorrow. My dad says that I will be able to see forever. I think I'll like that. Maybe I will be able to see my friend Gena's house back home. I will wave to her and shout hello. I'll hear the echo and pretend that she shouted back at me. But that is tomorrow, and my dad says that even the night is part of the journey. So I will close my eyes and listen for the owls, the wind in the trees, and the sound of my dad snoring. I love this place!

1. Do you think that there is anyone else in the family who is not on the hike? Explain your answer.

Answers will vary.

2. Do you think the narrator likes this trip? Why or why not?

Answers will vary.

3. Describe the setting.

They are hiking up a mountain in the summer.

Name

4.RI.3, 4.RI.6, 4.RI.10

Reading about Social Studies: Main Idea

Read the story. Then, answer the questions.

The Aztecs

The Aztec people lived in the area that is now central Mexico. The Aztec Empire lasted from about 1325 to 1521 and stretched from the Pacific Ocean to the Gulf of Mexico. The Aztecs had a strong central government that was headed by a king or emperor. Under him were officials who governed different parts of the empire. The Aztecs enjoyed many foods, including corn or maize, beans, squash, tomatoes, and chili peppers. People in Mexico still eat many of these foods today. The Aztecs built temples that were similar to the Egyptian pyramids but without the pointed tops. On the outside of the temples were steps to the top, where there was a flat area. The Aztec people are known for their pottery and statues. They also made beautiful feathered headdresses, masks, shields, and clothing for their rulers to wear and use. You can find examples of Aztec crafts in museums today.

1. What is the main idea of this story?
   a. The Aztec people lived in the area that is now called Mexico.
   (b.) The Aztecs had a strong government and made many crafts.
   c. Aztec temples are like the Egyptian pyramids.

2. How long did the Aztec Empire last?

It lasted for about 200 years.

3. How was the Aztec government organized?

It was a central government headed by a king or emperor

with officials under him who governed different parts of the

empire.

4. How are Aztec temples different from Egyptian pyramids?

Aztec temples have steps on the outside and do not have

pointed tops.

Name

4.RI.3, 4.RI.6, 4.RI.10

Reading about Social Studies: Main Idea

Read the story. Then, answer the questions.

World Holidays

People around the world celebrate different holidays. Both Canada and the United States have special days to mark the countries' birthdays. Canada Day is celebrated on July 1, and Independence Day in the United States is celebrated on July 4. On both of these holidays, people may have parades or picnics with their families. Many holidays have special foods associated with them. People may eat turkey on Thanksgiving or chocolate on Valentine's Day. During the Chinese Lantern Festival, people eat sticky rice dumplings. This holiday comes at the beginning of the Chinese New Year, in January or February, and has been celebrated for over 1,000 years! People in many other countries celebrate New Year's Eve on December 31. It is common for people to sing an old Scottish song called "Auld Lang Syne," which can be translated as "for old times' sake." They sing the song to remember the good times of the past and to look forward to more good times in the future.

1. What is the main idea of this story?
   a. Canada Day is celebrated on July 1.
   (b.) People around the world celebrate different holidays.
   c. Some people eat turkey at Thanksgiving.

2. How are Canada Day and Independence Day similar?

Both mark a country's birthday, both are celebrated in July,

and people celebrate in similar ways.

3. What are some foods eaten at holidays? **turkey, chocolate, sticky rice dumplings**

4. What festival is held at the Chinese New Year? **the Chinese Lantern Festival**

5. When is the Chinese New Year celebrated? When do other people celebrate the New Year?

the times include January or February; December 31

6. Why do people sing "Auld Lang Syne"?

This celebration is to remember the good times of the past

and to look forward to more good times in the future.

Answer Key

Name _____ 4.RI.3, 4.RI.6, 4.RI.10

Reading about Social Studies: Main Idea
Read the story. Then, answer the questions.

Becoming a U.S. State

There are 50 states in the United States today. The last states to be added were Alaska and Hawaii, in 1959. Most states admitted to the Union after the original 13 were U.S. territories first. To become a state, the people of the territory had to band together with an organized government and then write a state constitution. After the U.S. Congress accepted the constitution, that territory became a state. Areas that might become U.S. states someday include the island of Puerto Rico and the District of Columbia. While people who live in these areas now are U.S. citizens, they have limited voting rights. Puerto Rico has a resident commissioner instead of a senator, and the District of Columbia has a non-voting member of the U.S. House of Representatives. Each of the 50 U.S. states has two senators and one or more representatives in Congress. Some people who live in areas of the United States that are not states believe they need a greater say in Congress. Others would like to keep their independence.

1. What is the main idea of this story?

   Becoming a U.S. state allows people living there to have a

   say in the national government.

2. What were the last states to be added? When? **Alaska and Hawaii in 1959**

3. How does a U.S. territory become a state?

   The people living there form a government and write a

   constitution, which is then approved by the U.S. Congress.

4. How are U.S. territories different from U.S. states?

   People in U.S. territories do not send voting members to

   Congress.

5. How many members of Congress does each state have? **at least three**

6. Why might someone living in a U.S. territory want statehood?

   They can vote for members of Congress.

Name _____ 4.RI.1, 4.RI.2, 4.RI.10

Reading about Social Studies: Main Idea
Read the story. Then, answer the questions.

The Mississippi River

The Mississippi River is an important river for trade, recreation, and culture. It runs all the way from the U.S. state of Minnesota down to the Gulf of Mexico and covers 2,340 miles (3,770 km). The name Mississippi comes from an American Indian word meaning "great river." The first European explorer to reach the Mississippi was Hernando de Soto of Spain, who came there in 1541. In 1682 a group of French explorers claimed the river for their country. The city of New Orleans was built near the river in 1718. The United States acquired the area with the Louisiana Purchase of 1803. The Mississippi gained fame with the books of Mark Twain, which described life on the river. Twain, whose real name was Samuel Clemens, worked on a steamboat on the river in the late 1850s. Boats still travel down the Mississippi today, but people also water-ski and fish there. In addition, there are seven National Park Service areas along the river where people can go to enjoy nature.

1. What is the main idea of this story?
   a. The Mississippi River was made famous by Mark Twain.
   b. The Mississippi River was discovered by a Spanish explorer.
   c. The Mississippi River is important in many ways.

2. How long is the Mississippi?

   2,340 miles or 3,770 kilometers

3. Where did the Mississippi get its name?

   It is from an American Indian word meaning "great river."

4. Who was Samuel Clemens?

   He was an author who went by the name Mark Twain and

   worked on a steamboat on the Mississippi in the late 1850s.

Name _____ 4.RI.1, 4.RI.2, 4.RI.10

Reading about Social Studies: Main Idea
Read the story. Then, answer the questions.

The Field Museum

The Field Museum is a famous museum in Chicago, Illinois. It contains exhibits of animals, plants, and people from around the world. The museum was built in 1893. It was first called the Columbian Museum of Chicago because it contained the objects for the World's Columbian Exposition of that year. Its name was changed in 1905 to honor Marshall Field, who was an early supporter. The Field Museum contains the skeleton of "Sue," the world's largest and most famous Tyrannosaurus rex. Visitors can find out what Sue ate and how she lived. The buildings around the museum include the Shedd Aquarium, which has marine life from tiny sea horses to large sharks, and the Adler Planetarium, where people can find out information about stars and planets. Museum workers conduct research on not only how animals have lived in the past, but how we can save endangered species today. People who visit the museum enjoy seeing the exhibits, but they also like finding out how they can help.

1. What is the main idea of this story?
   a. People like visiting the Field Museum.
   b. The Columbian Museum of Chicago was built in 1893.
   c. The Field Museum has exhibits on many animals, plants, and people.

2. Why was the name of the museum changed?

   It was changed to honor an early supporter named Marshall

   Field.

3. Who is "Sue"?

   the world's largest and most famous Tyrannosaurus rex fossil

4. What can you see at the Shedd Aquarium?

   marine life

5. What are some things that museum workers do?

   They conduct research on how animals have lived in the past

   and how we can save endangered species today.

Name _____ 4.RI.1, 4.RI.2, 4.RI.10

Reading about Social Studies: Main Idea
Read the story. Then, answer the questions.

Family Trees

Have you ever heard of a family tree? A family tree is not a plant that grows in the park. It is a drawing that shows how everyone in your family is related. The branches of the tree show different parts of your family. Before you begin to create a family tree, you should find out the names of as many family members as you can. Research this by asking your relatives. Then, begin to draw your tree. Write your name in the middle. Next to your name, write the names of your siblings. Above your name, write the names of your parents or stepparents. Above each of their names, write the names of their parents. You may want to draw a picture of each person or use photographs. Building the tree together can be a fun activity for the whole family. You may find out you are related to someone famous!

1. What is the main idea of this story?

   A family tree shows how everyone in your family is related.

2. What do the branches of a family tree show?

   It shows different parts of your family.

3. Why should you talk to relatives about the family tree?

   because they will know names of people that you may not

   know

4. Where do you write your name on a family tree?

   in the middle

5. What goes above each name on a family tree?

   that person's parents or stepparents

6. What might you discover as you make your family tree?

   Answers will vary.

Answer Key

Name _____ (4.RI.3, 4.RI.6, 4.RI.9, 4.RI.10)

Reading about Social Studies: Main Idea
Read the story. Then, answer the questions.

The Economy

You may have heard your family or a newscaster discuss the economy. The economy is a system in which goods and services are exchanged for money. Goods are things that are produced, such as books and clothing. Services are things people do for each other. For example, a teacher provides the service of educating students, and a police officer provides the service of keeping the community safe. Sometimes people provide a service that produces a good, such as a cook who prepares a meal that you can eat. People pay money for goods and services. When you give money to a producer of goods, she can purchase materials to make more goods. When you give money to a service provider, he may pay for more training to do his job better. They can also use the money to pay for basic items such as food and shelter. When newscasters report that the economy is strong, it means that most people are happy with the amount of money, goods, and services they have.

1. What is the main idea of this story?
   a. Newscasters often talk about the economy.
   b. Sometimes the economy is strong, and other times it is weak.
   (c.) The economy is a system in which goods and services are exchanged for money.

2. What are goods?
   Goods are things that are produced.

3. List two examples of goods.
   Examples include books and clothing.

4. What is a service?
   Services are things people do for each other.

5. List two examples of service providers.
   A teacher educates students and a police officer keeps the community safe.

© Carson-Dellosa • CD-104622   29

Name _____ (4.RI.3, 4.RI.6, 4.RI.9, 4.RI.10)

Reading about Social Studies: Main Idea
Read the story. Then, answer the questions.

Citizen Rights and Responsibilities

People who are citizens of a country have certain rights that belong to them. These rights are sometimes listed in the laws of that country. In Canada and the United States, citizens over the age of 18 are given the right to vote. Citizens also have the right to a fair trial and the right to speak freely about what they believe. They can practice any religion they want to, and they have the right to gather peacefully to exchange ideas. They have the right to ask their government to change laws that they think are wrong. With these rights come responsibilities too. People should obey the laws of their country. They should respect the opinions of others, even if they disagree with them. They should help others in their community and try to protect their environment. It is important to remember that all citizens are part of a large community and that everyone deserves to be treated fairly.

1. What is the main idea of this story?
   (a.) All citizens of a country have rights and responsibilities.
   b. Citizens have the right to vote.
   c. Everyone should be treated fairly in a community.

2. Where can you find a list of citizens' rights? **in the laws of a country**

3. How old must citizens be to vote in Canada and the United States? **over the age of 18**

4. What are three rights in Canada and the United States?
   Answers will vary.

5. What are three responsibilities in Canada and the United States?
   Answers will vary.

6. Why is it important to treat all citizens fairly?
   Citizens are part of a large community and everyone should be treated fairly.

30   © Carson-Dellosa • CD-104622

Name _____ (4.RI.3, 4.RI.6, 4.RI.9, 4.RI.10)

Reading about Social Studies: Main Idea
Read the story. Then, answer the questions.

City Services

Cities provide many services to people who live there. The mayor and city council, who are elected by the citizens of that city, make the laws that everyone must follow. They also meet to discuss community issues, such as whether to build a new recreation center. Other city employees include police officers and firefighters. These people work to keep everyone in the city safe. Other city services are at the library, where the public can check out books, and at companies that provide water and electricity. Some cities have special programs for the people who live there, such as reading clubs at the library or computer classes for senior citizens. It takes many services to make a city work. Some people like to give back to their community by doing volunteer work. They might teach swimming lessons or offer to pick up litter in the parks. When everyone in a city works together, it can be a great place to live.

1. What is the main idea of this story?
   People living in a city receive many services.

2. Who elects the mayor and city council? **They are elected by the citizens.**

3. What do the mayor and city council members do?
   They make the laws everyone must follow and they meet to discuss community issues.

4. Name three employees who work for the city.
   Answers will vary.

5. What kinds of programs might a city have?
   A city may have reading clubs or computer classes.

6. How can people help their community?
   People can do volunteer work.

7. In what ways do you help your community?
   Answers will vary.

© Carson-Dellosa • CD-104622   31

Name _____ (4.RI.3, 4.RI.6, 4.RI.9, 4.RI.10)

Reading about Social Studies: Critical Thinking
Read the story. Then, answer the questions.

Tipi

For thousands of years, people have lived on the Great Plains of the United States and Canada. The Great Plains is a huge expanse of flat, grassy land with few trees. Many different animals used to roam on the plains. The groups of people who lived there would travel around and follow the animals to hunt. They needed homes that they could tear down and set up pretty quickly. Many Plains tribes, such as the Blackfoot, Sioux, and Cheyenne, built tipis to use as homes.

The first step in making a tipi was to find and prepare the poles. It took 15 poles to make just one tipi. The poles for the frame had to be long and straight. The best trees for this purpose were willow, pine, and cedar. The branches and bark were cut off so they did not poke holes in the tipi cover. When the people traveled with their homes, the poles dragged on the ground. The poles wore out and had to be replaced every year or two.

To prepare the buffalo hides, the women worked together on many steps. First, they scraped and cleaned the inside and outside of each hide. Then they soaked the hides with water to soften them. Next, they sewed as many as 14 hides together in the shape of a half circle. They cut a hole for the door and created smoke flaps. Finally, they fitted the cover over the frame and lit a fire inside. The smoke from the fire helped to preserve the skin. Some tipis were decorated with designs and symbols.

In the late 1800s, life on the Plains changed a lot. Many roads and cities began to fill the area. The buffalo were almost all gone. Many of the Plains people were forced to live on reservations. They no longer lived in tipis. Still, the tipi remains an important part of Native American culture today.

1. What are some tribes that live in the Great Plains?
   Tribes include the Blackfoot, Sioux, and Cheyenne.

2. Describe the poles needed to make a tipi.
   Fifteen long, straight poles stripped of branches and bark are needed for a tipi. They should be made from trees such as willows, pines, and cedars.

3. How did women prepare buffalo hides?
   They scraped, cleaned, and soaked the hides. They sewed hides together into a semicircle and cut a hole for the door and created smoke flaps. They fitted it over the frame.

32   © Carson-Dellosa • CD-104622

---

110   © Carson-Dellosa • CD-104622

Answer Key

Name _____ 4.RI.3, 4.RI.6, 4.RI.9, 4.RI.10

Reading about Social Studies: Critical Thinking
Read the story. Then, answer the questions.

The *Titanic*

The *Titanic* was one of the finest ships ever built. It was built to be comfortable and luxurious. What was life like on this expensive ship that only sailed on one voyage?

There were three levels of tickets. The most expensive tickets were for "first class." The next level was for "second class." The least expensive tickets were for those traveling in "third class" or "steerage."

The 329 "first-class" passengers had four decks on which to move around. They had cabins with sitting rooms. They could also visit with friends in several different lounges, restaurants, and dining rooms. They had a gym, a pool, a Turkish bath, a library, and beautiful sunny decks. Dinners consisted of many courses. First-class passengers could choose their meals from a menu. They ate at tables decorated with china plates, crystal, and fresh flowers. Some people wrote about what the ship was like. It was even fancier than what most rich people had at home.

The 285 "second-class" passengers were treated like the first-class passengers on other ships. They had nice cabins, but they were small. They ate a four-course meal each evening. They could also go on deck to walk around or sit in the sun. They did not have the restaurants, gyms, and other special rooms of the first class.

The 710 "third-class" passengers had space in the noisy rear of the ship below second class. There were only 220 cabins in "steerage." These cabins were used for families. The other passengers slept in large rooms. The men were in one room and the women were in a second room. The steerage sitting room was a large, plain room with benches and tables. Third-class passengers had to take turns eating in a dining room that sat only 473 people at a time. A ticket told them when to eat. If they missed their time, these passengers went hungry until the next meal.

Read the words of each passenger. Write whether the passenger is first-class (1), second-class (2), or third-class (3).

1 "I love my room. I have a beautiful bedroom with a private sitting room."

2 "My favorite meal is dinner when we have a delicious four-course meal."

1 "We swam for hours in the pool."

3 "In the evening, we sit on benches in the only room we all share. We play music and dance."

2 "I love to sit on the deck in the sun. My brother likes to play in the small cabin."

3 "We had to eat a little fast so the next group of people could come in and eat."

33

Name _____ 4.RI.3, 4.RI.6, 4.RI.9, 4.RI.10

Reading about Social Studies: Critical Thinking
Read the story. Then, answer the questions.

The *Mayflower*

Imagine leaving behind your home and all your things to sail across the ocean to a new world where there are no towns and no homes. This is what the passengers of the *Mayflower* faced in their journey from England to America in the year 1620.

The *Mayflower* traveled for 66 days across the unpredictable Atlantic Ocean. The ship carried 102 passengers and nearly 30 crew members. The passengers were the people who were riding on the boat from England to America. The sailors, or crew, were the people who worked on the ship. The crew planned to return to England once the passengers were settled.

Travel was difficult in rough weather. Passengers ate oatmeal, hard biscuits, dried fruit, rice, and salted beef brought with them from England. Many of the passengers became seasick during the trip. Occasionally, when the weather was calm, they would go up on deck to get fresh air and stretch their legs. The sailors preferred them to stay below and out of their way.

Every sailor was busy with the job of maintaining the ship. Some sailors climbed high on the mast to the lookout. Others put the sails up or down and repaired torn sails. Some sailors steered the boat. Others cooked for the crew in the forecastle. Many of the sailors helped to keep the boat clean. The sailors were paid well, but it was hard work.

When the ship landed in the Plymouth harbor, the passengers started the difficult task of settling in. They needed to build homes and get ready for the coming winter. Even the children had to work hard.

As soon as the passengers were settled, the crew of the *Mayflower* began the long, hard journey back to England.

1. Why do you think the sailors were paid so well? List three reasons.
   Answers will vary.

2. Why didn't the passengers go up on deck very often?
   The weather was rough. Many passengers were seasick.

3. How was the trip on the Mayflower different from a trip on a big ship today?
   Food: **There was less variety then and no refrigerators.**
   How the ship was powered: **The Mayflower used sails. Now, ships are powered with large engines.**

4. On a separate sheet of paper, write a paragraph explaining why you think life will be hard for the passengers in their new land. **Answers will vary.**

34

Name _____ 4.RI.2, 4.RI.10, 4.RF.4

Reading about Science: Main Idea
Read the story. Then, answer the questions.

Comets

Comets are objects that look like dirty snowballs flying through space. They have tails of dust that may be over 6 million miles (10 million km) long. Besides the tail, a comet has a nucleus, or center, made up of a closely packed ball of ice and dust. Surrounding the nucleus is a cloud of water and gases referred to as the coma. People can see comets only when they pass close to the sun. As they get closer to the sun, some of the ice in the nucleus melts, forming the long tail. Some comets appear after regular periods of time. Halley's Comet, named after Edmond Halley, the person who first predicted its return, passes through the solar system every 76 years. It was last seen in 1986 and will appear again in 2062. Earth is in no danger from comets. When the planet passes through the comet's tail, small pieces of rock called meteors fall into the atmosphere. Most of these are burned up in the mesosphere. They appear during a meteor shower as shooting stars.

1. What is the main idea of this story?
   a. Halley's Comet is very famous.
   (b.) Comets are objects from outer space made up of dust and ice.
   c. Comets are not dangerous to Earth.

2. Describe the parts of a comet.
   nucleus, or center—closely packed ball of ice and dust;
   coma—cloud of water and gases; tail—water and pieces of dust

3. What happens as a comet gets closer to the sun?
   Some of the ice in the nucleus melts, forming the long tail.

4. Who was Edmond Halley?
   He was the person who first predicted the comet's return.

5. What is a meteor?
   a. a comet that passes by every 76 years
   b. ice from the comet's nucleus
   (c.) a small piece of rock from space

35

Name _____ 4.RI.2, 4.RI.10, 4.RF.4

Reading about Science: Main Idea
Read the story. Then, answer the questions.

Plant Parts

Plants have many parts. You can see some of them, and there are parts you cannot see. The plant begins with the root system underground. It sends out long, thin roots into the soil to gather water and minerals. The part of the plant that grows out of the ground is called the stem. The stem moves water and minerals from the soil up into the leaves. Sunlight helps the leaves make more food, which is moved to other parts of the plant. The leaves also produce the oxygen in the air we breathe. Some leaves have only one broad, flat area connected to the stem. Others have many leaflets, or slim, needle-like parts. Many plants have flowers at the top of the stem. The petals of a flower help attract bees and butterflies, which bring pollen from other flowers. The pollen helps the flower make new plants the next year. Some plants produce fruit. When the seeds in the middle of the fruit are planted, a new plant can grow.

1. What is the main idea of this story?
   a. A plant's root system is underground.
   (b.) Plants have parts such as roots, leaves, and petals.
   c. Bees and butterflies like flowers.

2. How does the root system help the plant?
   It brings water and minerals from the soil to the stem.

3. What do leaves need to make food for the plant?
   water, minerals, and sunlight

4. Describe two ways that leaves can look.
   broad and flat or slim and needlelike

5. How do the petals of a flower help the plant?
   They attract bees and butterflies, which bring pollen.

6. What happens when seeds from fruit are planted?
   A new plant can grow.

36

Answer Key

Reading about Science: Main Idea

Read the story. Then, answer the questions.

Endangered Species

Many species of animals around the world are endangered today. This means that there are very few of them left. Species sometimes become endangered through loss of habitat, as when a wilderness area is changed by building a city there. They may also become endangered when people hunt them for food or for their skin. Many countries keep lists of the species that live there and are endangered. People can work to protect these species' environments from further loss. They can also move animals to zoos or nature preserves to try to increase their numbers. When they think it is safe again, they will reintroduce the animal to its native habitat. The alligator was once on the U.S. Endangered Species List because many people liked to make shoes or purses from its tough hide. After a law was passed making it illegal to kill alligators, the number of alligators in the wild increased. In 1987, it was removed from the list. The alligator is an endangered species success story!

1. What is the main idea of this story?
   Many species of animals around the world are endangered.

2. What does it mean for an animal to be endangered? **there are very few left**

3. How do species become endangered?
   The population shrinks due to habitat loss or overhunting.

4. How do people work to protect species?
   They protect their environments from further loss and move the animals to zoos or nature preserves.

5. When do people take animals back to their native habitat?
   when it is safe again or their numbers have increased

6. Why was the alligator removed from the U.S. Endangered Species List?
   Its numbers increased after a law was passed to make it illegal to kill alligators.

37

Reading about Science: Identifying Details

Read the paragraphs. Underline the sentence in each paragraph that tells its main idea. Highlight the details to support each main idea.

Primates

One reason to classify animals is to determine which ones are related to one another. Usually such classification is achieved by studying the skeletons and skins of the animal. Have you ever wondered to which animal you are related?

Monkeys and apes belong to a group called primates. (The word primate comes from a Latin word meaning first.) Monkeys and apes are called primates because they have complex brains. They are the most intelligent of all animals. Human beings are also classified as primates. Monkeys and apes have large brains like us and use their front limbs as hands. Monkeys, apes, and humans can think and use tools.

Early primates probably ate insects, but they also ate leaves and fruits. The chimpanzee is the most human looking of the primates. Although it eats mostly fruits, it will eat vegetables. It has even been seen eating insects and killing and eating small animals. Chimpanzees use sticks to get honey from a honeycomb or to dig ants and termites from their nests.

Check students' highlighting.

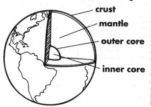

38

Reading about Science: Identifying Details

Read the following passage. Then, follow the directions.

Rattlesnakes

Rattlesnakes are poisonous reptiles whose home is anywhere from southern Canada in North America to Argentina in South America. There are 31 species of rattlesnakes. A large majority of them live in the southwestern United States and in Mexico.

A rattlesnake has excellent eyesight and a great sense of smell. Its forked tongue senses a combination of smells and tastes. It has ears but cannot receive outside sounds since an external and middle ear cavity are missing. It has an inner ear that enables it to detect ground vibrations.

fangs

rattle

The rattlesnake has two long teeth called fangs. The fangs inject a bitten animal with the snake's poison, called venom. Rattlesnakes hunt and eat rodents, small birds, lizards, and frogs whole. Because snakes digest food slowly, a rattlesnake may not hunt for several days.

The rattlesnake's rattle is probably its best known feature. It is a series of interlocking segments that vibrate whenever the tail shakes. When you hear its rattle, you do not want to go any closer.

Circle all of the facts that complete each sentence.

1. Rattlesnakes are _____ good pets (reptiles) (poisonous)
2. Rattlesnakes have _____ (fangs) (different colors) no ears
3. Rattlesnakes eat _____ (rodents) (small birds) humans
4. Rattlesnakes live in _____ (Mexico) (South America) Alaska
5. Rattlesnakes can _____ talk (see) (smell)

39

Reading about Science: Identifying Details

Read the story. Then, answer the questions.

How Earthquakes Happen

crust
mantle
outer core
inner core

Earth consists of four layers. The center is the core. The core consists of two parts: the inner and outer cores. The inner core is solid, and the outer core is liquid. The mantle surrounds the core. It is solid, hot rock. The crust covers the mantle. As the mantle moves around on the fluid of the outer core, it cracks the crust. The area of crust that breaks is known as a fault.

The cracked crust results in pieces of crust called plates. A plate is a large section of Earth's crust. The Earth's crust is made up of large and small plates. The plates are continually moving. Sometimes they bump, crunch, or move apart from each other. This movement eventually causes an earthquake.

In an earthquake, the ground moves back and forth and up and down. This movement may last seconds or a few minutes. When the shaking occurs, tall buildings can sway, pictures may fall off walls, and dishes may rattle. Fires may break out if the shaking causes underground gas lines to break. Lives may be lost. Earthquakes can cause a lot of damage.

1. Label the layers of Earth on the picture above.

2. What is a crack in the crust called? **fault**

3. Why might fires occur during an earthquake? **The shaking may cause underground gas lines to break.**

4. What causes an earthquake? **Earthquakes are caused by the movement of Earth's plates.**

5. What damage can an earthquake do? **Tall buildings can sway, pictures may fall off of walls, and dishes may rattle. Fires may break out and lives may be lost.**

40

Answer Key

Name _____ 4.RI.1, 4.RI.3, 4.RI.4, 4.RI.10

Reading about Science: Explaining Concepts
Read the story. Then, answer the questions.

Vaccinations

Some people go to the doctor for shots called vaccinations. Vaccinations can protect people and animals from diseases. The first vaccination was developed by Edward Jenner, who was looking for a way to prevent smallpox in the late 1700s. Vaccinations work by injecting a dead or weak part of the disease into a person or animal. The body makes antibodies to fight the disease, and the person or animal then becomes immune to that disease. This means that they will not develop the disease, or they will have only a very mild form of it. The most important animal vaccine is for the disease rabies. Many cities require that people vaccinate their pets so that none of them will catch the disease from a wild animal. Some people build natural antibodies to the diseases in their area. If you visit another country, you may be required to get a vaccination for a disease that exists in that country. People who live there might have natural antibodies to the disease, but a visitor might not. Vaccinations can help build antibodies to diseases with which you would not normally come into contact.

1. What disease was the first vaccination developed to prevent?

   smallpox

2. How do vaccinations work?

   A dead or weak part of the disease is injected and the body

   makes antibodies to fight the disease.

3. What does it mean to become *immune* to something?

   a. to get a shot at the doctor's office
   (b.) to have little chance of getting sick from a disease
   c. to visit another country

4. Why might you need a vaccination when you visit another country?

   because you might not have natural antibodies against the

   diseases found there

© Carson-Dellosa • CD-104622   41

Name _____ 4.RI.1, 4.RI.3, 4.RI.4, 4.RI.10

Reading about Science: Explaining Concepts
Read the story. Then, answer the questions.

Ecosystems

All living plants and animals live in ecosystems. An ecosystem can be as large as Earth or as small as a puddle. A lizard might live in a desert ecosystem. A whale might live in an ocean ecosystem. In an ecosystem, all of the living things, such as plants and animals, and nonliving things, such as the soil and the weather, work together. Changing even one thing will affect the other parts of the ecosystem. For example, if the ecosystem where frogs live becomes polluted, the frogs may become sick. If something happens to the frogs, then the animals that eat them, such as snakes, will not have enough food. If there is a fire in a forest, then the mosses on the forest floor will not have shade to grow in. The ecosystem will change from one with large trees and plants that need cool temperatures to one with plants that do well with more sunlight. People must try to protect the ecosystems in which they live. It is important to remember that even if you cannot see every organism in the ecosystem, everything is connected.

1. What is an ecosystem?

   a place where plants and animals live

2. Name three types of ecosystems.

   Answers will vary.

3. What happens if one thing is changed in an ecosystem?

   The other parts can change too.

4. What might happen if frogs in an ecosystem disappeared?

   The animals that eat them would have less to eat.

5. What might happen after a forest fire?

   The mosses on the forest floor would not have shade to grow

   in. The ecosystem would change into one with plants that

   need more sunlight.

42   © Carson-Dellosa • CD-104622

Name _____ 4.RI.1, 4.RI.3, 4.RI.4, 4.RI.10

Reading about Science: Explaining Concepts
Read the story. Then, answer the questions.

Biofuels

Gasoline is used in cars, and oil is used to heat many homes. Biofuels have similar uses, but they are made from things like vegetable oil, which can be recycled and used again. Diesel is a type of fuel similar to heating oil. Diesel fuel is used in cars and trucks. Biodiesel, most of which is made from soybean oil, burns more cleanly than diesel. It can be used in diesel engines without having to add any special parts. Biodiesel produces less pollution, so it is better for the environment. Gasoline is known as a fossil fuel, which means that it comes from layers deep under the earth that are made up of plants and animals that lived millions of years ago. Biofuel comes from plants we grow today, so it is a renewable resource. Some biofuels are created from restaurants' leftover grease that was used to make foods such as french fries or fried chicken. Instead of throwing this grease away, people are finding ways to power their cars with it.

1. What are biofuels?

   They are fuels made from things that can be recycled and

   used again.

2. Why might people choose to use biodiesel rather than diesel fuel?

   It burns more cleanly and is better for the environment.

3. What is a fossil fuel?

   fuel made from plants and animals from long ago

4. What is a renewable resource?

   It is something that can be used or grown again.

5. What are some things used to make biofuels?

   vegetable oil, soybean oil, and grease from fried foods

6. What do you think about using biofuel? Write your response below.

   Answers will vary.

© Carson-Dellosa • CD-104622   43

Name _____ 4.RI.2, 4.RI.4, 4.RI.10

Reading about Science: Vocabulary
Read the story. Then, answer the questions.

Volcanoes

Volcanoes are special mountains that sometimes shoot a hot liquid called lava into the air. Beneath a volcano is a pool of molten, or melted, rock. When the pressure underground builds up, the liquid is forced upward and out of the cone, or top, of the volcano. The liquid inside the volcano is called magma, but when it reaches the surface it is referred to as lava. A lava flow may travel down the sides of the volcano and over the land for several miles. As lava gets farther from the top of the volcano, it cools down and moves more slowly. Volcanic eruptions can be very harmful. Ash is sent into the air and can make it difficult to breathe. As lava gets farther from the eruption can flatten everything around the volcano, including forests and towns. Most volcanoes in the United States are located along the West Coast and in Hawaii and Alaska. The world's largest active volcano is in Mauna Loa, Hawaii. Another region of the world with many volcanoes is in the Pacific Ocean. This area is known as the Ring of Fire.

1. What is the main idea of this story?

   a. The Ring of Fire is located in the Pacific Ocean.
   (b.) Volcanoes shoot lava into the air and can be very dangerous.
   c. Lava flows can reach for miles around a volcano.

2. What is the cone of the volcano?

   (a.) the top, where lava shoots out
   b. the pool of molten rock underneath the earth
   c. the area around the volcano

3. What is the difference between magma and lava?

   Magma is liquid inside the volcano; it is called lava when it

   reaches the surface.

4. How can volcanoes be dangerous?

   They can shoot ash into the air, making it hard to breathe,

   and the rocks and lava can flatten forests and towns around

   the volcano.

44   © Carson-Dellosa • CD-104622

Answer Key

Name _____   4.RI.2, 4.RI.4, 4.RI.10

Reading about Science: Vocabulary

Read the story. Then, answer the questions.

Simple Machines

When you think of the word machine, you may picture a car engine or a lawnmower. These machines have many moving parts. Simple machines are tools that people use to make their work easier. They have very few parts. Instead of electric power, they use the energy of people to work. One simple machine is a lever. A lever is a board that rests on a turning point that makes it easier to lift things. A seesaw is a lever. Students on a seesaw use the board to make it easier to lift each other. Another simple machine is an inclined plane. To incline something means "to lean it against something else." An inclined plane is a flat surface that is higher on one end than the other. A ramp is an inclined plane. You might use a ramp to wheel a cart up to a curb instead of having to lift it. A slide is another inclined plane. Simple machines can make our lives easier in ways that are simple yet important.

1. What is the main idea of this story?
   a. Car engines and lawnmowers have many parts.
   b. A seesaw is a type of simple machine.
   c. Simple machines can make our lives much easier.

2. What do simple machines use instead of electricity?
   They depend upon the energy of people.

3. What is a lever?
   It is a board that rests on a turning point that makes it easier to lift things.

4. What does it mean to incline?
   a. lean at an angle
   b. use a simple machine
   c. play on a seesaw

5. What is an inclined plane?
   It is a flat surface that is higher on one end than the other.

© Carson-Dellosa • CD-104622   45

Name _____   4.RI.2, 4.RI.4, 4.RI.10

Reading about Science: Vocabulary

Read the story. Then, answer the questions.

Atoms and Molecules

Everything around you is called matter—from your chair to your clothes to your family. Matter is made up of atoms and molecules, which are very tiny building blocks. Atoms make up chemical elements, such as the oxygen in the air you breathe. Atoms are combined to create molecules, such as the water you drink. Atoms are composed of even smaller particles called protons, neutrons, and electrons. A proton has a positive charge, an electron has a negative charge, and a neutron has no charge. The protons and neutrons stay together in the nucleus, or middle, while the electrons orbit, or move around, the atom. The number of protons determines the type of atom that is formed. Hydrogen is the simplest atom. It has only one proton. Oxygen has eight protons. Together, hydrogen and oxygen can form a molecule of water. Each water molecule has two hydrogen atoms and one oxygen atom. A glass of water contains too many molecules to count!

1. What is the main idea of this story?
   All matter is made up of atoms and molecules.

2. What are two examples of atoms?
   oxygen, hydrogen

3. What does orbit mean?
   move around something

4. Describe the differences between protons, neutrons, and electrons.
   protons—positive charge, stay in nucleus; neutrons—no charge, stay in nucleus; electrons—negative charge, orbit nucleus

5. Why is hydrogen the simplest atom?
   It has only one proton.

6. What is a water molecule made up of?
   Water has two hydrogen atoms and one oxygen atom.

46   © Carson-Dellosa • CD-104622

Name _____   4.RI.4, 4.RI.7, 4.RI.10

Reading about Science: Visual Aids

Read the following information. Then complete the chart.

Mollusks

Mollusks belong to a large family of invertebrate animals. Animals that belong to this group usually have soft, one-sectioned bodies that are covered by hard shells. A person walking on a beach might find discarded shells. We think of them as seashells, but once an animal lived in them.

Biologists divide mollusks into seven groups called classes, but only some of them have hard protective shells. Gastropoda is one class of mollusks. Most gastropods have a single, coiled shell. Included in this class are slugs, snails, and whelks. They can be found on the beaches of the Atlantic and Pacific Oceans in North America.

Bivalves is another large class of mollusks. The shells of bivalves are two shells hinged together at one end or along one side. The animals that call these shells home include clams, mussels, and scallops. They, too, can be found on both coasts of North America.

A third class of mollusks are chitons. Their bodies are covered by eight shell plates that look like a turtle's shell. Merten's chiton, northern red chiton, and mossy mopalia are all included in this class. Chitons live in shallow rock pools. They are found along the Pacific Ocean from Alaska to Mexico.

	gastropods	bivalves	chitons
What do their shells look like?	single, coiled shell	two shells hinged together at one end or along one side	eight shell plates that look like a turtle's shell
Where can they be found?	beaches of Atlantic and Pacific Oceans in North America	both coasts of North America	along the Pacific Ocean from Alaska to Mexico, shallow rock pools
List mollusks included in each class.	slugs snails whelks	clams mussels scallops	Merten's chiton northern red chiton mossy mopalia

© Carson-Dellosa • CD-104622   47

Name _____   4.RI.4, 4.RI.7, 4.RI.10

Reading about Science: Visual Aids

Read the story. Then, follow the directions.

The Brain

The brain is an organ of the body that controls almost everything the human body does. It is divided into three parts. Each part controls different bodily functions. The three parts are the medulla, the cerebellum, and the cerebrum.

The medulla is located where the spinal cord enters the head. It takes care of involuntary actions. Involuntary actions do not require any decision making. Breathing, digestion, and elimination are examples of involuntary actions.

Voluntary acts demand some instruction. Brushing one's teeth, dressing, or turning a somersault are examples of voluntary actions. The cerebellum is the part of the brain that controls bodily movement.

The largest part of the brain is the cerebrum. It controls voluntary mental operations such as the senses, muscles, speech, thinking, remembering, learning, and deciding. The cerebrum is divided into two equal parts called hemispheres. The hemispheres are covered by a layer of nerve cells called the cortex. There are many centers located in different areas of the cortex that send and receive messages. Each of the operations the cerebrum controls is located in a different center.

Write each word or phrase in the diagram to show the main idea and its supporting ideas.

a. involuntary actions
b. parts of the brain
c. cerebellum
d. medulla
e. cerebrum
f. voluntary movements
g. voluntary mental operations

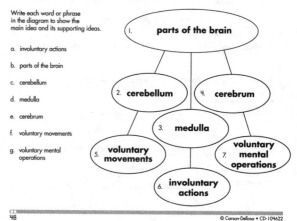

48   © Carson-Dellosa • CD-104622

Answer Key

Name _____ 4.RI.4, 4.RI.7

Reading about Science: Visual Aids
Read the story and diagram. Then, answer the questions.

Dinosaurs lived long ago—about 60 million years ago. Today all that is left of them are their fossils, bones, and footprints. But what does 60 million years mean to someone your age? A geologic time scale was developed by scientists that illustrates the periods in Earth's history. It can help those of us living today gain some perspective about the time involved in the development of life on Earth.

GEOLOGIC AND EVOLUTIONARY TIME SCALE

1. Earth's history is divided into how many major eras?
four

2. What are their names?
Cenozoic, Mesozoic, Paleozoic, Precambrian

3. In which era did the dinosaurs exist?
Mesozoic

4. How many periods is the Mesozoic era divided into?
three

5. What are their names?
Cretaceous, Jurassic, Triassic

6. In how many of these periods did dinosaurs live?
all

7. In what era do you live?
Cenozoic

© Carson-Dellosa • CD-104622   49

Name _____ 4.RI.1, 4.RI.2, 4.RI.10

Reading about Symbolism
Read the story. Then, answer the questions.

Smiley Face

You have probably seen a bright yellow smiley face in an ad or on a sign. Some people even wear them on T-shirts! The smiley face was created in 1963 by an artist named Harvey Ball. Ball was asked to come up with a symbol for an insurance company to use. The company wanted employees to feel cheerful about working for the company when they saw the smiley face. Ball drew something very simple and made the background yellow because it reminded him of the sun. Soon, the symbol became so popular that thousands of people outside the company were wearing smiley face buttons. In the 1970s, the smiley face was put on T-shirts, coffee mugs, and bumper stickers. It has brought a smile to many people's faces around the world. Today, people sometimes use smiley faces in their e-mails to represent different feelings. Harvey Ball probably never thought his symbol would still be used over 40 years later.

1. What is the main idea of this story?
   a. The smiley face is still used today.
   b. Harvey Ball created the smiley face.
   c. The smiley face is a simple symbol that has been around for a long time.

2. Why was the smiley face created?
An artist created the symbol for employees of an insurance company.

3. Why did Harvey Ball make the background yellow?
because it reminded him of the sun

4. How was the smiley face used in the 1970s?
It was put on T-shirts, coffee mugs, and bumper stickers.

5. How do people use the smiley face today?
They use smiley faces in their emails to represent different feelings.

50   © Carson-Dellosa • CD-104622

Name _____ 4.RI.1, 4.RI.2, 4.RI.10

Reading about Symbolism
Read the story. Then, answer the questions.

Colors

Colors can symbolize different things. When you see the color orange, you might feel happy because it reminds you of a sunny day. It might make you feel warm. When you see the color blue, you might feel calm because it makes you think of a still lake. It might make you feel cool to think of swimming in the water. When you see the colors green, brown, and blue together, you might think of the beauty of nature. These colors are used on world globes. Colors can also be used on courageous. Fire trucks are red so that people will notice them and move out of the way. Stoplights use colors to tell cars whether to move. A red light signals to stop, a green light signals to go, and a yellow light signals to yield, or to slow down and be more careful. Pay attention to the colors around you. They might help you in ways you do not expect.

1. What is the main idea of this story?
   a. Colors can mean many different things.
   b. A still lake might make you feel calm.
   c. Pay attention to the colors around you.

2. What does the color orange make you think of?
Answers will vary.

3. What does the color blue make you think of?
Answers will vary.

4. Why might green, brown, and blue make you think of nature?
Answers will vary.

5. Why are fire trucks red?
so people will notice them and move out of the way

6. What do the colors on a stoplight mean?
red—stop; green—go; yellow—slow down and use caution

© Carson-Dellosa • CD-104622   51

Name _____ 4.RI.1, 4.RI.2, 4.RI.10

Reading about Symbolism
Read the story. Then, answer the questions.

Political Parties

Political parties are groups of people who feel the same way about one or more issues. Each party may work to elect several candidates to office, from the president down to the city mayor. Political parties often use symbols to represent them. When people see that symbol, they will think of the party. The donkey was first used in a political ad to represent President Andrew Jackson, who was a Democrat. Donkeys can be smart and courageous. The U.S. Republican Party symbol is the elephant. Elephants are known for their strength and intelligence. Both of these parties use red, white, and blue—the colors of the U.S. flag. Many of the Canadian political parties have maple leaves as part of their logos, or designs. The maple leaf appears on the Canadian flag, so this shows that the parties are tied to their country. Political parties in Great Britain use different symbols. The Labor Party uses the rose (the national flower), the Conservative Party uses the oak tree (for strength), and the Liberal Democrats use a dove (for peace).

1. What is the main idea of this story?
Political parties use symbols to represent them.

2. What are political parties? **groups who feel the same way about issues**

3. Why does the Democratic Party use a donkey?
Answers will vary.

4. Why does the Republican Party use an elephant?
Answers will vary.

5. Why might a political party use symbols from its country's flag?
Answers will vary.

6. What are some symbols used by British political parties? **rose, oak tree, dove**

7. What is an issue you feel strongly about?
Answers will vary.

52   © Carson-Dellosa • CD-104622

Answer Key

Reading about Symbolism
Read the story. Then, answer the questions.

Country Flags

Each country of the world uses a different flag. The flag tells something special about that country. It may have colors that are important to that country's people. It may have a picture of an important animal. The flag of the United States has 13 stripes and 50 stars. The stripes represent the original 13 colonies, and the stars stand for the 50 states in the country today. The flag of Canada has a maple leaf. There are many maple trees in Canada. The red leaf is shown on a white band between two bands of red.

1. What is the main idea of this story?
   a. The Canadian flag has red and white areas.
   b. A flag may have animals on it.
   c. Flags tell something special about a country.

2. Why does each country have its own flag?
   to tell something special about that country

3. What things might you find on a flag?
   colors, plants, or animals

4. What do the stripes and stars represent on the U.S. flag?
   The stripes stand for the original 13 colonies, and the stars
   stand for the current 50 states.

5. What does the maple leaf mean on the Canadian flag?
   There are many maple trees in Canada.

Reading about Symbolism
Read the story. Then, answer the questions.

Coats of Arms

A coat of arms is a special design used by a family or another group to show something special about that group. Coats of arms were used by knights in the Middle Ages to identify themselves. This design might be passed down through a family. A coat of arms often has an area called a "shield" in the middle. The shield may have different shapes or colors. Around the shield, there may be animals such as lions or eagles. Above the shield, there may be a special saying, such as "Knowledge and Honor." Countries sometimes use coats of arms as well. The Great Seal of the United States has many of the same elements as a coat of arms. It shows a bald eagle holding 13 arrows in one claw and an olive branch with 13 leaves in the other. The number of arrows and leaves stand for the 13 original states. The seal is used on important papers. It also appears on the U.S. one-dollar bill.

1. What is the main idea of this story?
   a. A coat of arms often has a shield on it.
   b. Coats of arms can stand for a family or another group.
   c. The Great Seal appears on the U.S. dollar bill.

2. What is a coat of arms?
   It is a special design used by a family or group to show
   something special about that group.

3. How were coats of arms used in the Middle Ages?
   They were used by knights to identify themselves.

4. What different things might appear on a shield?
   Answers will vary.

5. What might appear above the shield? **a special saying**

6. Describe the Great Seal of the United States.
   It shows a bald eagle holding 13 arrows in one claw and an
   olive branch with 13 leaves in the other.

Reading about Symbolism
Read the story. Then, answer the questions.

What Are Symbols?

Symbols are things that stand for other things. We use symbols such as letters to stand for the sounds we make when we speak. The words made up by the letters stand for ideas. A symbol can tell how you feel about something. Your school might have a symbol such as a lion or a panther stand for its teams. When you think of that animal, you feel pride in your school. Some symbols are used to stand for bigger things. The flag is a symbol of your country. A TV station might use a symbol to show the channel its programs are broadcast on. You can also see symbols in many buildings. Symbols help you know which restroom to use and which doors are accessible to people that use wheelchairs. These symbols are used as a kind of shorthand so that you can see the picture and quickly know what it means. Symbols are important in our everyday lives.

1. What is the main idea of this story?
   Symbols are important to our lives.

2. What are symbols?
   things that stand for other things

3. Where might you see a symbol?
   Answers will vary.

4. Why might a school team use an animal as a symbol?
   Answers will vary.

5. Why might a TV station use a symbol?
   to show the channel its programs are broadcast on

6. Why are symbols important?
   Answers will vary.

7. Design your own symbol to represent yourself on a separate sheet of paper.
   Designs will vary.

Reading about Symbolism
Read the story. Then, answer the questions.

Birthday Symbols

Many people recognize their birthdays by doing something special, such as inviting their friends over or having a family dinner. There are also special symbols that stand for the different months of the year, such as flowers and gemstones. Each of these also has a meaning connected with it. For example, the flower for March birthdays is the daffodil. This yellow flower represents happiness and friendship. The flower was chosen because it blooms during that month. Gemstones are another way of recognizing different birthday months. These pretty, sparkling rocks are polished and used to make jewelry. People might wear earrings, a necklace, or a pin with their birthstone in it. The gemstone for January is the deep red garnet stone. May's birthstone is an emerald, which is bright green. The most famous birthstone is probably the diamond, which stands for the month of April. On your next birthday, remember your special flower and gemstone too.

1. What is the main idea of this story?
   a. Stones and flowers always stand for the same thing.
   b. The daffodil is the flower for March.
   c. Each month has a special flower and stone.

2. What does the daffodil stand for?
   happiness and friendship

3. How are birthday flowers chosen?
   They are chosen based on the flowers blooming that month.

4. What are gemstones?
   a. polished rocks used in jewelry
   b. special kinds of flowers
   c. stones that are dull and gray

5. What do garnets and emeralds look like?
   Garnets are deep red and emeralds are bright green.

Answer Key

Reading about Symbolism

Read the story. Then, answer the questions.

Flowers to Remember

Many countries have special days to remember different people. These days have special flowers connected with them as well. Mother's Day is celebrated in Canada and the United States on the second Sunday in May. Many people give carnations to their mothers on Mother's Day. The flower for Grandparents' Day, which is celebrated on the first Sunday after the U.S. Labor Day, in September, is a forget-me-not. These flowers are small and blue and have a yellow center. Another special day is Veterans Day. On this U.S. holiday, people honor the soldiers who have served in the military. In Canada, this holiday is Remembrance Day, because people *remember* those who have served. Both of these holidays are observed on November 11 every year. In Canada, people wear poppies on their coats. Poppies are red flowers with a black middle. The flowers stand for the poppies that bloomed over a French battlefield during World War I.

1. What is the main idea of this story?
   a. Some people wear poppies on their coats.
   (b.) Different flowers are worn on special holidays.
   c. Special days help us remember different people.

2. When is Mother's Day celebrated in the United States and Canada?
   on the second Sunday in May

3. What flowers are used for Mother's Day and Grandparents' Day?
   Carnations are used for Mother's Day and forget-me-nots are
   used for Grandparents' Day.

4. What does *remembrance* mean? **remembering someone or something**

5. When are Veterans Day and Remembrance Day celebrated? **November 11**

6. What do the poppies worn on Remembrance Day stand for?
   the poppies that bloomed over a French battlefield during
   World War I

Reading about Symbolism

Read the story. Then, answer the questions.

Symbols of Canadian Provinces

While Canada has many national symbols, such as the loon and the maple leaf, each of its provinces also has special symbols to represent it. Many of them have provincial plants, animals, and mottoes, or sayings. The province of Newfoundland and Labrador even has its own song! Alberta's official flower is the wild rose, and its bird is the great horned owl. Its motto is "strong and free," and its provincial fish is the bull trout. New Brunswick's flower is the purple violet. Its bird is the black-capped chickadee, and its tree is the balsam fir. Nova Scotia's official animal is a dog called the duck-tolling retriever. Its name means that it is good at finding ducks. Manitoba's bird is the great gray owl. Its official animal is the bison, and its tree is the white spruce. The province's motto is "glorious and free." Each province also has its own flag to show something about the history of that area.

1. What is the main idea of this story?
   Canadian provinces use symbols to tell something about them.

2. What is a *motto*?
   a short saying that represents an idea

3. What is special about the province of Newfoundland and Labrador?
   It has its own provincial song.

4. List the provincial flowers for two Canadian provinces.
   Alberta—wild rose; New Brunswick—purple violet

5. What does a provincial flag tell you about that province?
   It tells you about the history of the area.

6. Develop your own motto. Write it below.
   Answers will vary.

Reading about Symbolism

Read the story. Then, answer the questions.

The Loon

The loon is the state bird of Minnesota (United States) and the provincial bird of Ontario (Canada). Loons can be found in the northern part of the United States and throughout most of Canada. A loon is about the size of a large duck and has a dark head and checkered gray and white feathers. Loons dive for fish in lakes as deep as about 200 feet (61 m) under the surface. They can swim for long distances underwater. Loons fly south to Mexico in the winter and come back north when the ice melts in the spring. In 1998, the Canadian postal service issued a special stamp worth one dollar that had a picture of a loon on it. The loon also appears on the Canadian dollar coin, which was introduced in 1987. This coin is often called the loonie. The Canadian two-dollar coin, introduced in 1996, features a polar bear. People call this coin the toonie.

1. What is the main idea of this story?
   (a.) Loons are special birds in Canada.
   b. Loons dive for fish underwater.
   c. The Canadian dollar coin is called the loonie.

2. Which U.S. state and Canadian province honor the loon?
   Minnesota and Ontario

3. Where are loons found?
   in the northern part of the United States and throughout
   Canada

4. What does a loon look like?
   It is the size of a large duck and has a dark head and
   checkered gray and white feathers.

Reading about Symbolism

Read the story. Then, answer the questions.

U.S. State Symbols

The United States has many national symbols that represent liberty and freedom. Each U.S. state also has its own symbols, including state animals, flowers, and flags. The state of Washington has a picture of George Washington, the first U.S. president, on its flag. The state fruit is the apple, and the state vegetable is the Walla Walla sweet onion, which grows in the city of Walla Walla. Louisiana has a pelican, the state bird, on its flag. The state reptile is the alligator. Alaska's flag shows a pattern of stars known as the Big Dipper. The state fish is the king salmon, and the state mineral is gold. Ohio's state insect is the ladybug. The state tree is the buckeye, and the state beverage is tomato juice. Texas is known as the Lone Star State because its flag has a single star on it. The state plant is the prickly pear cactus, and the state flower is the bluebonnet. Each state's symbols can tell you a lot about the plants and animals that live there.

1. What is the main idea of this story?
   a. National symbols represent liberty and freedom.
   (b.) U.S. states have many different symbols.
   c. The state tree of Ohio is the buckeye.

2. What are the state bird and reptile of Louisiana?
   The state bird is a pelican, and the state reptile is an alligator.

3. What does the Alaska flag look like?
   It has a pattern of stars known as the Big Dipper.

4. Why is Texas called the Lone Star State?
   Its flag has a single star on it.

5. What do a state's symbols tell you about it?
   They tell you about the plants and animals that live there.

Answer Key

Reading about Symbolism

Read the story. Then, answer the questions.

Animal Symbols

Animals can mean different things to different people. To one family, a squirrel might be just a pest in the yard, but to another, a squirrel might serve as a reminder to put away food for the winter. A lion represents strength and courage, but it also stands for the country of Great Britain. It appears on the country's official coat of arms and reminds people of King Richard the Lionheart. The eagle stands for freedom, strength, and courage. It appears on the Great Seal of the United States and is also important in many American Indian cultures. Sports teams often choose an animal to represent them on the playing field. The team members remember their animal's qualities, such as speed and power, when they are playing. Some cars are also named after animals, such as a mustang or a ram, so that people will think the cars are as fast or as strong as those animals.

1. What is the main idea of this story?

Animals are important symbols for different groups of people.

2. How might people see squirrels differently?

Some people see them as pests, while some are reminded to put away food for the winter.

3. What does the lion stand for? **strength and courage**

4. What does the eagle stand for? **freedom, strength, and courage**

5. Why might a sports team choose an animal to represent it?

To represent them on the playing field and so the members can remember that animal's qualities when they are playing.

6. Why are some cars named after animals?

so people will think the cars are like the animals

Compare and Contrast

Read the diagram. Then answer the questions.

WHAT HAVE YOU READ?

Venn diagram. Left circle "Rivers Flow Steadily": Brendan, Trey, Keisha, Natalie, Ben, Young, Juan, Spenser, Nathan. Center overlap: Polly, Jay, Kelly, John, Ritu. Right circle "When the Mountains Call": Evelyn, Phillip, Pia, Ahmed, Stacy, Jim, Elena.

1. How many children have read *Rivers Flow Steadily*? **12**

2. How many children have not read *Rivers Flow Steadily*? **9**

3. How many children were questioned? **21**

4. Which children have not read either book?

Trey, Brendan, Evelyn, and Phillip

5. How many children have read *When the Mountains Call*? **10**

6. Which children have read both books?

Polly, Jay, Kelly, John, and Ritu

Compare and Contrast

Read the passage. Then, follow the directions.

Elephants

There are two kinds of elephants living today, the Indian elephant and the African elephant. The Indian elephant is smaller, stands about ten feet tall, and weighs about four tons. It has smaller ears, a high forehead, and only one lip at the end of its smooth trunk. There are five nails on each of its front feet and four on each hind foot. Only the male has small tusks. The Indian elephant is usually the one seen in zoos. The African elephant is around eleven feet tall, and weighs about six tons. Its ears are big, and its forehead is sloped. Its front feet each have four nails, and the hind feet each have three nails. Also, its trunk is ringed, and its tusks are large.

Compare the two kinds of elephants by filling in the chart below. First, write the names of the two kinds of elephants on the top lines. Then fill in their vital statistics. If the information was not given in the article, fill in the blank with "not given."

1. Elephants	**Indian elephant**	**African elephant**
2. Height:	10 feet	11 feet
3. Weight:	4 tons	6 tons
4. Ears:	small	big
5. Forehead:	high	sloped
6. Lips:	one lip	not given
7. Skin on trunk:	smooth	ringed
8. Tusks:	only on males, small	large
9. Nails:	five on front, four on hind	four on front, three on hind

---

Compare and Contrast

The men in the passage below have had similar and yet different lives. Read the passage about them. Then, underline three facts in blue that show the differences between the players. Underline three facts in red that show their likenesses.

Michael Jordan and Kareem Abdul-Jabbar

Michael Jordan grew up in North Carolina. His father built a basketball court in the backyard for all his children to use. Michael enjoyed all sports, but basketball was his favorite. Jordan tried to make his high school's varsity team, but the coach thought he was too short. However, by his junior year he had grown and sharpened his basketball skills, and he made the high school team. The rest is history: getting a scholarship to the University of North Carolina, winning the national championship for the University, helping the U.S. Olympic basketball team win a gold medal, and becoming a Chicago Bull. Michael Jordan broke many National Basketball Association (NBA) records and received several Most Valuable Player (MVP) awards. He retired from basketball and tried baseball, but after two years away from basketball, he returned and set even more records.

Kareem Abdul-Jabbar was born Ferdinand Lewis Alcindor, Jr. He was born and raised in the New York City area. Early on, he had a passion for music and baseball. He played in Little League and was a pitcher for his junior high school. Not until the summer between first and second grade did he first pick up a basketball. In eighth grade he led his junior high to win the district championship. Lew made the high school varsity team his freshman year and the rest is history: leading his high school to record-setting winning streaks, receiving a scholarship to the University of California at Los Angeles, and leading the team to three titles while receiving three MVP awards. During his college years he changed his name to Kareem Abdul-Jabbar. He also boycotted the 1968 Olympics. He and other U.S. athletes decided a boycott would send a message about racism in the U.S. After college he was drafted by the Milwaukee Bucks and then traded six years later to the Los Angeles Lakers. For both teams he had personal and team successes. He was voted MVP five times. He was the NBA's leading scorer and led both teams to national championships.

Answers will vary.

Answer Key

Determining Meaning

> Some words have more than one meaning. You can tell which meaning is being used from the context of the sentence.
>
> Examples: The ticket taker **admitted** Alan into the theater after the movie started.
> Here, admitted means permitted or allowed.
>
> Nancy **admitted** she had not done her homework.
> Here, admitted means confessed or acknowledged.

Circle the correct definition for the underlined word.

1. Perry was wearing an <u>olive</u> shirt with a tan skirt and socks.
   - a fruit
   - (a color)
   - an evergreen tree

2. The police arrested the driver at the scene of the accident and <u>booked</u> him for reckless driving.
   - (entered charges against)
   - made reservations
   - printed pages bound together in a volume

3. The horse <u>bolted</u> from the barn during the heavy rainstorm.
   - a rod to fasten a door
   - a roll of cloth
   - (darted off; dashed)

4. After the long hike, Mike saw the beginning of a blister on his <u>sole</u>.
   - the only one
   - a flat fish
   - (the bottom of the foot)

5. Mary stood <u>erect</u> and went for shelter when she heard the tornado warning.
   - (straightness in bodily posture)
   - build
   - set up or establish

6. We walked several blocks before we were able to <u>hail</u> a taxi.
   - icy precipitation
   - (signal)
   - greet with enthusiasm

7. Mom had to <u>tramp</u> through the snow to reach the mailbox.
   - a person with no fixed home
   - (to step heavily)
   - shovel

8. The <u>light</u> in the corner of the room flickered just before it burned out.
   - not heavy
   - (lamp)
   - brightness

Determining Meaning

> At times you may not recognize a word in a sentence or know its meaning, but there are ways to figure it out. One is by its part of speech. Example: The carpet's colors **harmonize** with those of the walls and furniture. Decide what part of speech the underlined word is, what function it has in the sentence, and what it actually means.
>
> Another way is to use the other words in the sentence. Example: The team was **forlorn** after losing the game. The other words tell you that the team was sad.

Use context clues to choose the correct word. Write it on the blank.

1. _____**Astronomy**_____ is one of Tom's favorite subjects. (Astronaut, Astronomy, Atmosphere)

2. He _____**especially**_____ liked to follow the movement of the stars. (especially, establish, exceptionally)

3. Tom was delighted when his family gave him a _____**telescope**_____ for his birthday. (telegram, telephoned, telescope)

4. Part of his birthday present was also to go camping with his father to a park where _____**conditions**_____ were good for stargazing. (constellations, conditions, conjunctions)

5. When the night came for Tom to go to the park, he took the necessary equipment with which to make his _____**observations**_____. (observes, orbits, observations)

6. Tom saw several _____**constellations**_____ including Orion and the Dippers. (consultants, constellations, confirmations)

7. He drew pictures of what he saw and recorded their positions using a _____**compass**_____. (compass, confess, congress)

8. He had a wonderful time and asked if his father would take him on another _____**expedition**_____ to observe the stars. (explore, expedition, experience)

Determining Meaning

Space Science

The Space Age began in 1957 when the United Soviet Socialist Republics (U.S.S.R.) <u>launched</u> the first satellite named Sputnik I. Though the satellite was very small, the importance of its mission <u>transformed</u> how the world is able to look at space. Sputnik I was the first object to go beyond Earth's <u>atmosphere</u>. Since then thousands of satellites have been launched, mostly by the <u>former</u> U.S.S.R. and the United States. Today the satellites are much larger and heavier. Some weigh several tons, and their <u>payloads</u> have a purpose related to the design of each satellite's <u>mission</u>. Today's satellites are designed to perform different tasks, including exploring Earth and space, observing the weather, improving communications, and assisting the military.

Until the Space Age there were <u>theories</u> about space, but they could not be proven. They could only be <u>evaluated</u> from observations and using instruments on the ground. The atmosphere that surrounds Earth <u>distorts</u> the way the stars really look because of the substances within the atmosphere. By putting satellites beyond Earth's atmosphere, scientists can get a better picture of distant stars and perhaps the <u>universe</u>.

Use context clues to choose the meaning for each underlined word above. Write the underlined word next to its definition.

1. the layers of gases surrounding Earth **atmosphere**
2. initiated; released **launched**
3. determined; tested **evaluated**
4. a specific task **mission**
5. changed **transformed**
6. twists normal shape **distorts**
7. before in time **former**
8. beliefs; analyses of a set of facts **theories**
9. everything in an entire space system **universe**
10. loads carried by a satellite necessary for the flight **payloads**

Multiple Meanings

> Many words have more than one meaning. Sometimes you can figure out the correct meaning by seeing how the word is used in a sentence.

Read the sentences below. Circle the correct meaning for the underlined word in each sentence.

1. She offered a <u>concrete</u> suggestion on how to create a plan.
   - a. made of cement
   - (b. solid)

2. The large candle gave off a <u>brilliant</u> light.
   - a. very smart
   - (b. very bright)

3. My <u>goal</u> is to become a famous scientist someday.
   - (a. ambition)
   - b. points scored in some sports

4. The <u>patch</u> of pumpkins grew very well.
   - (a. area of land)
   - b. scrap of cloth

5. When a storm is coming, my cat acts very <u>odd</u>.
   - a. number that is not even
   - (b. unusual)

6. It is sometimes hard to be <u>patient</u>.
   - (a. calm about waiting)
   - b. ill or injured person

7. It took several tries at walking before the baby felt <u>stable</u> on her feet.
   - (a. steady)
   - b. place where horses are kept

Answer Key

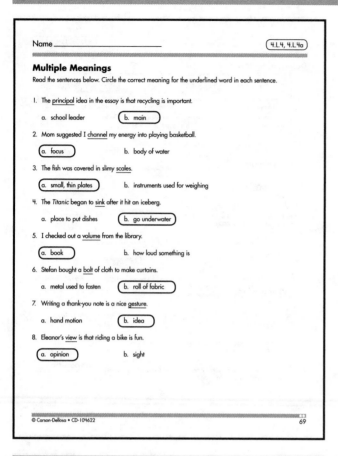

Multiple Meanings

Read the sentences below. Circle the correct meaning for the underlined word in each sentence.

1. The principal idea in the essay is that recycling is important.
   - a. school leader
   - **b. main**

2. Mom suggested I channel my energy into playing basketball.
   - **a. focus**
   - b. body of water

3. The fish was covered in slimy scales.
   - **a. small, thin plates**
   - b. instruments used for weighing

4. The *Titanic* began to sink after it hit an iceberg.
   - a. place to put dishes
   - **b. go underwater**

5. I checked out a volume from the library.
   - **a. book**
   - b. how loud something is

6. Stefan bought a bolt of cloth to make curtains.
   - a. metal used to fasten
   - **b. roll of fabric**

7. Writing a thank-you note is a nice gesture.
   - a. hand motion
   - **b. idea**

8. Eleanor's view is that riding a bike is fun.
   - **a. opinion**
   - b. sight

Multiple Meanings

Read the sentences below. Circle the correct meaning for the underlined word in each sentence.

1. The sailor took the vessel out to sea.
   - a. part of the body that moves blood
   - **b. ship**

2. The football player weaved through the other people on the field.
   - **a. moved in a zigzag manner**
   - b. sewed cloth

3. The plot of the film was unusual.
   - **a. storyline**
   - b. area of land

4. The beam from the powerful flashlight lit every corner.
   - a. plank of wood
   - **b. light**

5. Please do not tread on the flowers.
   - **a. step heavily**
   - b. part of a tire

6. The mayor proposed a new plan to control traffic.
   - **a. suggested**
   - b. asked someone to marry

7. The glare from the sun hurt our eyes.
   - a. frown
   - **b. bright light**

8. Larry was the sole winner of the spelling bee.
   - a. part of the foot
   - **b. only**

9. All of his limbs were sore after he completed the race.
   - a. tree branches
   - **b. arms and legs**

Multiple Meanings

Read the sentences below. Circle the correct meaning for the underlined word in each sentence.

1. We hailed a cab to go home after the play.
   - a. ice from the sky
   - **b. called for**

2. The tone of the film was joyful.
   - a. sound or vibration
   - **b. mood**

3. Do you know who coined the phrase "to each his own"?
   - a. turned into money
   - **b. made up**

4. My brother hatched a plan to finish his homework and see the movie too.
   - **a. thought of**
   - b. came out of an egg

5. Many members of royalty have titles like "emperor" or "queen."
   - **a. words that come before names**
   - b. phrases that describe a book

6. We are having a major test on Friday that covers three chapters.
   - a. person in the armed forces
   - **b. important**

7. Paulo was not present when the guest speaker came to school.
   - a. gift
   - **b. in attendance**

Multiple Meanings

Read the sentences below. Circle the correct meaning for the underlined word in each sentence.

1. My stepdad says my mom is the anchor of our family.
   - **a. strong support**
   - b. metal weight on a ship

2. The referee gave the signal to begin the game.
   - **a. motion**
   - b. traffic light

3. Mom made sure the picture frame was level before hanging it on the wall.
   - **a. even on both sides**
   - b. flat and smooth

4. As the tomatoes grew bigger, they began to swell.
   - a. excellent
   - **b. grow in size**

5. Mrs. Chin used a baton to conduct the band.
   - **a. direct or guide**
   - b. behave in a certain way

6. It took me a few hours to recover after the long hike.
   - a. put new cloth over something
   - **b. feel better**

7. I wrote an outline before starting my essay.
   - a. drawing around
   - **b. list of important points**

8. Milk will not last very long if you leave it outside in hot weather.
   - **a. remain fresh**
   - b. the end of something

Answer Key

Name _____ (4.L.4, 4.L.4a)

Multiple Meanings

Read the sentences below. Circle the correct meaning for the underlined word in each sentence.

1. My aunt often works the night shift at her job.
   - (a. period of time)
   - b. to change or move

2. We stopped to pay a toll when we crossed the bridge.
   - (a. slight charge)
   - b. sound of a bell

3. The Olympic swimmer reached his peak during his best event.
   - a. mountaintop
   - (b. best point of performance)

4. Lan's pants had a trace of dirt on them.
   - (a. small mark)
   - b. to draw around something

5. Every time a truck goes by, it jars our living-room windows.
   - a. pots
   - (b. rattles)

6. I kept dwelling on my teacher's kind words after class.
   - (a. thinking about)
   - b. living place

7. Olivia thought she could spy a squirrel in the treetop.
   - a. secret agent
   - (b. glimpse)

8. A U.S. senator's term of office is six years.
   - a. word or phrase
   - (b. length)

9. Before my dog was trained, his behavior was too rough.
   - (a. rowdy or forceful)
   - b. bumpy or jagged

© Carson-Dellosa • CD-104622   73

Name _____ (4.RF.3, 4.RF.3a, 4.L.4)

Word Analysis Skills: Prefixes

> A **prefix** comes at the beginning of a word.

Look at the words below. Write new words by adding re- before each. The prefix re- means "to do something again." Use the new words to fill in the blanks in the sentences below.

claim	**reclaim**
consider	**reconsider**
fuel	**refuel**
turn	**return**
tell	**retell**
cycle	**recycle**

1. After school is out, I will **return** to my house for the day.
2. After speaking to her coach, Josie will **reconsider** her decision to quit the team.
3. Mom stopped at the gas station to **refuel** her car on her way to work.
4. Our family tries to **recycle** products so that less trash goes into the landfill.
5. My neighbor came to **reclaim** his lost dog.
6. Uncle Joe likes to **retell** his favorite joke over and over again.

74   © Carson-Dellosa • CD-104622

Name _____ (4.RF.3, 4.RF.3a, 4.L.4)

Word Analysis Skills: Prefixes

Look at the words below. Write new words by adding un- before each. The prefix un- is used to make something into its opposite. Use the new words to fill in the blanks in the sentences below.

aware	**unaware**
important	**unimportant**
safe	**unsafe**
lock	**unlock**
like	**unlike**
cover	**uncover**
affected	**unaffected**

1. It can be **unsafe** to ride your bicycle barefoot.
2. Kirby was **unaware** that the plan for the weekend had changed.
3. I used my key to **unlock** the door.
4. The parade was **unaffected** by the dark clouds.
5. After I make my bed, I will **uncover** my pillow.
6. That painting is **unlike** any other I have seen.
7. Dad says it is **unimportant** whether I am tall or short.

© Carson-Dellosa • CD-104622   75

Name _____ (4.RF.3, 4.RF.3a, 4.L.4)

Word Analysis Skills: Prefixes

Look at the words below. Write new words by adding re- before each. The prefix re- means "to do something again." Use the new words to fill in the blanks in the sentences below.

fill	**refill**
build	**rebuild**
wire	**rewire**
new	**renew**
read	**reread**
do	**redo**
appear	**reappear**
write	**rewrite**

1. An electrician will **rewire** the fan to make it work.
2. After the teacher looks at our rough drafts, we will **rewrite** our papers.
3. The flowers in the garden are gone, but they will **reappear** next spring.
4. I need to **renew** my membership before it expires.
5. Jim had to **redo** his poster after it got wet in the rain.
6. Dad will **rebuild** the doghouse now that our puppy has grown.
7. I enjoyed the book so much that I am going to **reread** it.
8. I asked Mom if I could **refill** my drink.

76   © Carson-Dellosa • CD-104622

Answer Key

Name _____   4.RF.3, 4.RF.3a, 4.L.4

Word Analysis Skills: Prefixes

A **prefix** comes at the beginning of a word.

Look at the words below. Write new words by adding un- before each. The prefix un- is used to make something into its opposite. Use the new words to fill in the blanks in the sentences below.

usual	**unusual**
limited	**unlimited**
common	**uncommon**
friendly	**unfriendly**
certain	**uncertain**
able	**unable**

1. When I was walking to school this morning, I saw an **unusual** sight.
2. It is **uncommon** to have snow here in October.
3. Her uncle was **uncertain** whether he could attend the play.
4. If it is raining tomorrow, we will be **unable** to run the relay.
5. At first, the girl seemed **unfriendly** but it turned out she was just shy.
6. We had **unlimited** trips to the buffet during the all-you-can-eat lunch.

Name _____   4.RF.3, 4.RF.3a, 4.L.4

Word Analysis Skills: Prefixes

Look at the words below. Write new words by adding under- before each. The prefix under- means "to be below another thing" or "to not have enough of something." Use the new words to fill in the blanks in the sentences below.

stand	**understand**
taking	**undertaking**
cooked	**undercooked**
brush	**underbrush**
water	**underwater**
foot	**underfoot**
cover	**undercover**

1. The detective went **undercover** to solve the mystery.
2. This project is a large **undertaking** but I know we can handle it.
3. The diver explored the **underwater** caves.
4. My dog always seems to be **underfoot** when I am trying to walk.
5. Uncle Kieran thought the bread was ready to eat, but it was **undercooked**.
6. I **understand** how to do the most difficult math problems.
7. Dad cleared away the **underbrush** from our backyard.

Name _____   4.RF.3, 4.RF.3a, 4.L.4

Word Analysis Skills: Prefixes

Look at the words below. Write new words by adding after- before each. The prefix after- means "to come after or later than something." Use the new words to fill in the blanks in the sentences below.

noon	**afternoon**
effect	**aftereffect**
taste	**aftertaste**
image	**afterimage**
glow	**afterglow**
thought	**afterthought**
shock	**aftershock**
care	**aftercare**

1. After the operation, the nurses provided **aftercare** to the patient.
2. The **aftereffect** of running the race was that I was tired the next day.
3. After looking at the bright stadium lights, the player saw an **afterimage** each time he blinked.
4. The **afterglow** from the fireworks lit the sky for a moment.
5. After an earthquake, a city may have an **aftershock**.
6. Adding fresh strawberries was an **afterthought** but they made the pancakes taste great!
7. The spicy food left a strong **aftertaste** in my mouth.
8. Every **afternoon** I play with my friends down the street.

Name _____   4.RF.3, 4.RF.3a, 4.L.4

Word Analysis Skills: Prefixes

A **prefix** comes at the beginning of a word.

Look at the words below. Write new words by adding be- before each. The prefix be- means "on or around" or "to cause something to happen." Use the new words to fill in the blanks in the sentences below.

fore	**before**
side	**beside**
low	**below**
come	**become**
cause	**because**
ware	**beware**

1. Jamal said he liked the movie **because** it was funny.
2. The sign said to **beware** of snakes on the trail.
3. There are roses growing **below** my bedroom window.
4. It is important to study **before** a test.
5. Cherie hopes to **become** an author one day.
6. Pattie sits **beside** her best friend, Kara.

Answer Key

Name

4.RF.3, 4.RF.3a, 4.L.4

Word Analysis Skills: Prefixes

Look at the words below. Write new words by adding over- before each. The prefix over- means "to go above or have too much of something." Use the new words to fill in the blanks in the sentences below.

flow	**overflow**
due	**overdue**
night	**overnight**
sight	**oversight**
looked	**overlooked**
heat	**overheat**
cast	**overcast**

1. The bucket started to **overflow** after it had rained all week.
2. If you **overheat** the roast, it will be too dry.
3. My friends and I are planning an **overnight** slumber party.
4. When the clouds hid the sun, the sky was **overcast**.
5. My library books will be **overdue** if I do not turn them in today.
6. The mistake in that book was an **oversight**.
7. Miss Gomez **overlooked** my name the first time she read the list.

© Carson-Dellosa • CD-104622   81

Name

4.RF.3, 4.RF.3a, 4.L.4

Word Analysis Skills: Prefixes

Look at the words below. Write new words by adding out- before each. The prefix out- means "to go beyond." Use the new words to fill in the blanks in the sentences below.

come	**outcome**
last	**outlast**
look	**outlook**
put	**output**
spoken	**outspoken**
run	**outrun**
wit	**outwit**
numbered	**outnumbered**

1. Tina was able to **outrun** everyone else in the race.
2. The presidential candidates each had a different **outlook** on taxes.
3. Their team **outnumbered** ours by five people.
4. My aunt is quite **outspoken** about her ideas on recycling.
5. I hope to **outlast** the other students during the spelling bee.
6. In the story, the clever hen was able to **outwit** the fox.
7. Jared was pleased with the **outcome** of his baseball game.
8. Our **output** has increased since we started working as a team.

82   © Carson-Dellosa • CD-104622

Name

4.RF.3, 4.RF.3a, 4.L.4

Word Analysis Skills: Suffixes

> A **suffix** comes at the end of a word.

In the sentences below, choose the word with the correct suffix for each blank.

1. My puppy is learning to **behave**. Her **behavior** is very good. (behave, behavior)

2. We asked our teacher to **approve** our project. She thought it was a great idea and gave us her **approval**. (approve, approval)

3. Raul could not believe his good **fortune**. He thought he was **fortunate** to be chosen as the lead in the class play. (fortunate, fortune)

4. My aunt is known for her **organization**. She can **organize** even the most cluttered closet. (organization, organize)

5. Please **indicate** your interest in the club by signing the list. Your name is an **indication** that you want to join. (indicate, indication)

6. My sister and I do not look very **similar**. Our one **similarity** is that we both have blonde hair. (similarity, similar)

© Carson-Dellosa • CD-104622   83

Name

4.RF.3, 4.RF.3a, 4.L.4

Word Analysis Skills: Suffixes

In the sentences below, choose the word with the correct suffix for each blank.

1. My best **friend** is Consuela. She is **friendly** to everyone. (friend, friendly)

2. Steve would like to be a **teacher**. He wants to **teach** either social studies or art. (teach, teacher)

3. The painting was a **magnificent** work of art. Its **magnificence** was known throughout the world. (magnificence, magnificent)

4. The principal will make an important **announcement** this afternoon. She will **announce** the winners of the school poster contest. (announcement, announce)

5. Earth is part of the vast **universe**. Gravity is a **universal** scientific law. (universe, universal)

6. Shanika's piano playing will **astonish** the crowd. Their **astonishment** will be great. (astonishment, astonish)

7. Our soccer team was **victorious**. Our coach led us to **victory**. (victory, victorious)

84   © Carson-Dellosa • CD-104622

Answer Key

Word Analysis Skills: Suffixes

In the sentences below, choose the word with the correct suffix for each blank.

1. I have great **admiration** for my mother. Many other people **admire** her too. (admire, admiration)

2. Juan is the most **patient** person I know. He has **patience** even with his little brothers. (patience, patient)

3. Mrs. Han likes working in **management** She can **manage** any project she tries. (management, manage)

4. Thomas Edison was a great **inventor** He liked to **invent** new things in his workshop. (inventor, invent)

5. Sometimes I **hesitate** before making a decision. My **hesitation** means that I am thinking about it. (hesitate, hesitation)

6. The **brilliance** of the light could be seen for miles. The light had a **brilliant** glow. (brilliant, brilliance)

7. I take **frequent** breaks when studying for a test. The **frequency** of my breaks decreases as I begin to understand the material better. (frequency, frequent)

8. The radio station's **transmission** reaches for many miles. The station can **transmit** to several different cities. (transmission, transmit)

Writing Skills

Read the story. Then, follow the checklist to use what you learned to write a research paper.

The Tundra

The tundra is a special type of land found in extremely cold areas such as the Arctic and parts of Alaska and Canada. The tundra is sometimes referred to as a frozen desert. In areas with tundra, the ground is frozen the whole year. This permanently frozen ground is called permafrost. Very short shrubs grow in the tundra. It is difficult for taller plants to grow because the ground is so cold and hard. The tundra can be very windy because there is so little to block the wind. Wind speeds can reach nearly 60 miles (about 100 kilometers) per hour. Few animals live in the tundra because there are not many plants. However, many birds and insects travel there in the summertime when the ice on the marshes and lakes melts. Because of the cold, windy conditions, it is difficult for people to live in areas with tundra. Some scientists work on research stations for part of the year to study the plants and animals that live there.

Writing Checklist

_____ 1. Research the tundra using a computer.

_____ 2. Find two websites with credible information. Write them below.

_____

_____

_____ 3. Type a minimum of one page of information about the topic.

_____ 4. Review your work and make revisions with peer editors.

Answers will vary.

Writing Skills

Read the story. Then, follow the checklist to use what you learned to write a research paper.

The Atmosphere

The atmosphere is the air that surrounds Earth. The air you breathe is part of the atmosphere. Earth's atmosphere contains the gases oxygen, nitrogen, and argon, along with dust, pollen, and water. Oxygen is the most important part of the atmosphere. It is made by plants during their food-making process. In addition to breathing the atmosphere, you can also feel it. When you feel a cool breeze in autumn or warm air on a summer day, you are feeling the atmosphere. The atmosphere has different layers. The troposphere is the layer above the surface of Earth. The troposphere makes up half the atmosphere. All weather occurs in this layer. The next layer is the stratosphere, where jets often fly. This layer absorbs much of the sun's harmful rays. In the mesosphere, the third layer of the atmosphere, rocks from space are caught and burned. The space shuttle orbits in the next layer, the thermosphere. The last layer is the exosphere. After that, you are out in space!

Writing Checklist

_____ 1. Research Earth's atmosphere using your computer.

_____ 2. Find three websites with credible information. Write them below.

_____

_____

_____

_____ 3. Type a minimum of one page of information about the topic.

_____ 4. Review your work and make revisions with peer editors.

Answers will vary.

Writing Skills

Read the story. Then, follow the checklist to use what you learned to write a research paper.

Climate

The climate describes the weather in an area over a long period of time. If you live somewhere where there are large amounts of yearly rainfall, then you live in a rainy climate. If your town is very hot and dry, then you may live in a desert climate. Some cities, such as San Diego, California, have a very mild climate. Others, such as New Orleans, Louisiana, have warm, heavy air, so they have a humid climate. While the weather in a place may change from day to day, a region's climate seldom changes. Factors other than weather can also affect the climate in a given area. Areas that are close to the sea are cooler and wetter. They may also be cloudy, because clouds form when warm inland air meets the cooler air from the sea. Mountains may also affect climate. Because the temperature at the top of a mountain is cooler than at the ground level, the mountaintop may have year-round snow. Regions near Earth's middle, or equator, are warmer than those at the poles. Sunlight has farther to travel to get to the north and south poles, so these areas are much cooler.

Writing Checklist

_____ 1. Research climate using your computer.

_____ 2. Find four websites with credible information. Write them below.

_____

_____

_____

_____

_____ 3. Type a minimum of one page of information about the topic.

_____ 4. Review your work and make revisions with peer editors.

Answers will vary.

Answer Key

Name _____ 4.W.2, 4.W.6, 4.RF.4

Writing Skills

Read the story. Then, follow the checklist to use what you learned to write a research paper.

Reading Maps

Have you ever used a map to plan a route? A world map shows the outlines of the continents and seas. It may have parts shaded brown and green to show areas of desert or forest. A city map shows important buildings such as the library or city hall, as well as city streets. Maps use symbols to help you understand them. A compass rose looks like an eight-pointed star inside a circle. It shows you the directions north, south, east, and west. North is usually at the top. A map scale tells you how distances on the map relate to the real world. For example, one inch (2.5 cm) on the map may be equal to 100 miles (160.9 km). A map legend shows you what other symbols mean. A black dot may stand for a city, a star inside a circle may mean a country's capital city, and an airplane may be used to represent an airport. Knowing what these symbols mean makes it much easier to travel.

Writing Checklist

_____ 1. Research maps using your computer.

_____ 2. Find two websites with credible information. Write them below.

_____

_____

_____ 3. Type a minimum of one page of information about the topic.

_____ 4. Review your work and make revisions with peer editors.

Answers will vary.

Name _____ 4.W.2, 4.W.6, 4.RF.4

Writing Skills

Read the story. Then, follow the checklist to use what you learned to write a research paper.

Rainbows

You may have seen a rainbow in the sky after a rainstorm. A rainbow includes the colors red, orange, yellow, green, blue, indigo, and violet. You can remember the order of the colors with the name Roy G. Biv. All of the colors combined create white light. A rainbow is formed when a ray of sunlight shines through a cloud, refracts off the water droplets, and is split into bands of color. Rainbows are fairly rare to see. This is because special conditions are required for them to become visible. To see a rainbow, you must have rain in front of you, at a distance, and the sun behind you, low on the horizon. The curve of the rainbow is in the direction opposite from the sun. Rainbows are more common in summertime, because you must have both rain and warm sunlight to see them. Because there is less sunlight and more frozen water, rainbows are less likely to form during winter.

Writing Checklist

_____ 1. Research rainbows using your computer.

_____ 2. Find three websites with credible information. Write them below.

_____

_____

_____ 3. Type a minimum of one page of information about the topic.

_____ 4. Review your work and make revisions with peer editors.

Answers will vary.

Name _____ 4.W.2, 4.W.6, 4.RF.4

Writing Skills

Read the story. Then, follow the checklist to use what you learned to write a research paper.

Salmon

Animals such as dogs and cats may spend their entire lives in the same city or town in which they were born. Other animals, however, travel great distances during their life cycle. The salmon swims from the rivers of Alaska to the Pacific Ocean and back again. The salmon lays its eggs in the riverbed. After about three months, the eggs hatch. Then, the tiny fish swim around the rivers until they are large enough to travel to the sea. As the fish grow older and larger, they develop patterns that look like finger marks along their sides. Once they are one to three years old, they move in groups toward the ocean. Their bodies change so they can live in salt water instead of freshwater. The young salmon then spend several years swimming in the ocean. Eventually, they will swim back to the river in which they were born. There they lay eggs, and the cycle begins again.

Writing Checklist

_____ 1. Research salmon using your computer.

_____ 2. Find four websites with credible information. Write them below.

_____

_____

_____

_____ 3. Type a minimum of one page of information about the topic.

_____ 4. Review your work and make revisions with peer editors.

Answers will vary.

Name _____ 4.L.1, 4.L.3

Nouns

A **noun** is a word that names a person, place, or thing.

Read the story below. Some of the nouns are missing. Fill in the blanks with the words from the word box below.

apartment	brother	students	art	family
library	place	state	teacher	notice
school	work	mother	club	projects

Raven and her little **brother** needed a new **place** to go after school. They usually went to their aunt's **apartment**, but she was moving to another **state**.

Raven's **mother** did not finish **work** early enough to pick them up at school.

Raven saw a **notice** at **school** about a new **club** that was forming. It was for **students** aged eight to ten. They would meet after school, walk to the **library** with the art **teacher**, and work on art **projects** until someone from their **family** could come get them. Raven thought that was perfect! She loved **art**, and so did her brother. She could not wait to tell Mom.

Answer Key

Worksheet 1 (page 93)

Nouns

Read the story below. Some of the nouns are missing. Fill in the blanks with the words from the word box below.

topic	something	class	model	magnets
salad	science	planets	system	friends
advice	stepdad	project	plants	garden
ideas	tomatoes			

Stefani needed to choose a creative **project** for science **class**. First, she wanted to study **magnets**. She could show how to pull them apart. Then, she thought she would build a **model** of the solar **system**. She could show how the different **planets** moved. Finally, Stefani thought about growing tomato **plants**. She liked working in the **garden**. Stefani had many good **ideas**. She asked her **stepdad** which **topic** to choose. He said, "Pick **something** that the whole family will enjoy." Stefani thought that was great **advice**. She decided to grow **tomatoes**. She could make a tasty **salad** when she was done! Her project for **science** was delicious. She wanted to share it with her **friends**.

Worksheet 2 (page 94)

Nouns

Read the story below. Some of the nouns are missing. Fill in the blanks with the words from the word box below.

mother	suit	hills	weekend	dad
neighborhood	park	socks	pavement	store
hobby	morning	lunchtime	block	shoes
family	treadmill	sister		

Lakshmi's **dad** loved to run. He ran down the streets in their **neighborhood** every **morning** before sunrise. Then, he ran once around the **block** at **lunchtime**. He also ran up and down the steep **hills** by the city **park** each **weekend** morning. Lakshmi thought this **hobby** looked like fun. She asked her dad if she could run with him. Dad said, "Sure!" He took Lakshmi to the **store** to buy a track **suit** and **socks** that would keep her feet dry. Finally, they bought running **shoes**. Now Lakshmi's older **sister** wants to run too! Soon, her whole **family** will be running. Her **mother** wanted to give it a try. She practiced on the **treadmill** on the weekend. She is ready to hit the **pavement**.

Worksheet 3 (page 95)

Verbs

A **verb** is a word that tells what kind of action is being performed.

Read the story below. Some of the verbs are missing. Fill in the blanks with the words from the word box below.

fry	like	picks	tastes	stop
arrive	buy	helps	wait	take
have	wake	brings	puts	cast

Benny and his sister Hannah **like** to go fishing with their uncle. They **wake** up early on a Saturday morning. Uncle Ray **picks** them up in his old pickup truck. He **brings** fishing rods and an icebox. They **stop** to **buy** bait and cold drinks on the way to the lake. When they **arrive**, Uncle Ray **puts** the bait on the hook. He **helps** Benny and Hannah **cast** their lines into the water. Then, they **wait** for a fish to **take** the bait. Soon they **have** enough fish for dinner. They **fry** the fish with vegetables. It **tastes** great!

Worksheet 4 (page 96)

Verbs

Read the story below. Some of the verbs are missing. Fill in the blanks with the words from the word box below.

laugh	watch	showed	dressed	sounded
went	were	felt	looked	smiled
felt	loved	called	knew	was
play	cheered			

Keesha **loved** to **watch** her older sister, Kendra, **play** volleyball. She **dressed** in the colors for Kendra's school and **went** to all of the games. She **cheered** until she **sounded** hoarse. Kendra **called** Keesha her biggest fan. Keesha **felt** sad that she **was** too small to play volleyball. Kendra and the rest of her teammates **were** very tall. One day Keesha's mom **showed** her a picture of Kendra when she was Keesha's age. Kendra **looked** just like Keesha did now. Keesha **smiled** and started to **laugh**. "Kendra was small once too! Maybe I can play volleyball one day after all." Keesha **felt** proud of herself. She **knew** she could do it!

Answer Key

Name _____   4.L.1, 4.L.3

Verbs

Read the story below. Some of the verbs are missing. Fill in the blanks with the words from the word box below.

gets	walk	has	walked	loves
started	turned	exercise	stepped	would
does	walks	trusts	works	opened
called	come	running		

Kamran **has** a new after-school job. His neighbor, Mr. Quigley, just **started** coaching soccer in the evenings, and he **does** not have time to **come** home after work. Mr. Quigley said he **trusts** Kamran to **exercise** his dog, Leo. Kamran **walks** Leo to the park and back before he **works** on his homework. On the first day of Kamran's new job, he **opened** the gate and **called** Leo's name. Leo came **running**. He was ready for his walk! As Kamran and Leo **walked** down the street, another neighbor, Mrs. Pellini, **stepped** out of her house. She asked, "Kamran, **would** you **walk** my dog too? Katie **loves** to go to the park." Now Kamran **gets** twice the exercise! His after-school job **turned** into a business and a workout routine.

Name _____   4.L.1, 4.L.3

Adjectives

> An **adjective** is a word that describes something.

Read the story below. Some of the adjectives are missing. Fill in the blanks with the words from the word box below.

enormous	beautiful	dark	quiet	awful
better	great	inspiring	fine	sad
nervous	cheerful	deep	bright	shaky

My choir director, Mrs. Rosas, is an **inspiring** person. She helps us memorize **beautiful** songs so that we can give a **fine** performance. When I tried out for the choir, I was very **nervous**. My voice was **quiet** and **shaky**, and I thought that I sounded **awful**. Mrs. Rosas smiled and said she knew that I could do a **better** job. She told me to take a **deep** breath and try the song again. This time I sounded **great**! Our choir wears **bright** red shirts with **dark** pants when we sing. Being in the choir makes me feel **cheerful**. If I am **sad** when I start singing, by the end of the song I have an **enormous** smile on my face again.

Order of adjectives may vary.

Name _____   4.L.1, 4.L.3

Adjectives

Read the story below. Some of the adjectives are missing. Fill in the blanks with the words from the word box below.

marvelous	wonderful	older	fun	favorite
lengthy	yellow	giant	surprised	nice
closest	fabulous	special	front	long
happy	blue			

Leticia and her **older** brother, Amos, wanted to plan a **wonderful** surprise party for their mom. She always threw parties for them that were **fabulous** and **fun**. Now it would be her own **special** day. Leticia made a **long** list of all of her mom's **closest** friends. Mom was such a **nice** person, everyone wanted to be her friend. Amos ordered a **giant** cake with **blue** and **yellow** icing to feed all of the guests. These were Mom's **favorite** colors. On the day of the party, Leticia asked Mom to go on a **lengthy** walk. When they got home, all of Mom's friends were hiding in the living room. When Mom opened the **front** door, they all shouted, "Surprise!" Mom said it was the most **marvelous** party ever. She felt **surprised** and very **happy**.

Order of adjectives may vary.

Name _____   4.L.1, 4.L.3

Adjectives

Read the story below. Some of the adjectives are missing. Fill in the blanks with the words from the word box below.

famous	long	vast	slender	longer
brilliant	creative	green	deep	enormous
dark	tiny	best	whole	great
detailed	proud	exciting		

Angelica decided to write a book. She loved to read, and her teachers said that she had a **great** imagination. Her heroine would have **green** eyes and **long**, **dark** hair, just like Angelica. She would live in the middle of a **vast**, **deep** forest. Angelica imagined the animals that might come to visit her character— **enormous** bears, **slender** deer, and **tiny** mice. She worked on her **creative** story every day at lunchtime and after school. It grew **longer** and soon took up a **whole** notebook! Angelica let her **best** friend, Mindy, read her story. Mindy thought it was **brilliant** and very **detailed**. She said she could not wait until Angelica was a **famous** author one day! Mindy felt **proud** of her friend. She loved reading Angelica's **exciting** stories.

Order of adjectives may vary.

Answer Key

Name _____   4.L.1g, 4.L.3, 4.L.4

Homophones

> **Homophones** are words that sound alike but are spelled differently and have different meanings.

Write the correct homophone on the line.

1. ____**No**____, you may not have any candy before dinner.

2. I don't ____**know**____ what street Julio lives on.

3. There are ____**no**____ dogs allowed here.

no: antonym of yes

know: verb, to understand

4. Julian has a ____**new**____ bike.

5. Willow ____**knew**____ where Paco lived.

6. The ____**new**____ theater has comfortable seats.

new: not old

knew: verb, past tense of know

7. Put your name in the upper ____**right**____ corner.

8. Please ____**write**____ your name on the paper.

9. Yes, that answer is ____**right**____.

write: verb, to make purposeful marks, for example with a pencil

right: to be correct or a direction opposite of left

10. We are not ____**allowed**____ to chew gum in school.

11. When you read ____**aloud**____, it bothers me.

12. Are we ____**allowed**____ to bring pets to school?

allowed: permitted

aloud: out loud

Name _____   4.L.1g, 4.L.3, 4.L.4

Homophones

After each sentence below are two homophones. Write the homophone that makes sense in the sentence on the line. Write a sentence using the other homophone on the line.

1. The ____**bough**____ of the tree hung low over the sidewalk. (bough, bow)

2. Jane had been sick for over a week and was ____**bored**____ staying in bed. (board, bored)

3. The wranglers watched the ____**herd**____ on the range. (heard, herd)

4. Dick and Tom passed ____**through**____ the passage that led into the cave. (threw, through)

5. An ____**ark**____ is a type of boat. (ark, arc)

6. In ____**which**____ shop did you find your new shoes? (witch, which)

7. Father stopped and asked the ____**way**____ to the stadium. (way, weigh)

8. The campers put a ____**grate**____ over the fire and put water on it to boil. (great, grate)

Sentences will vary.

Name _____   4.L.1g, 4.L.3, 4.L.4

Homophones

Read each sentence and choose the set of homophones from the list below that belongs. Write the correct homophone on each line. Not all the homophone sets will be used.

capital	threw	heal	grays	principle	patience
capitol	through	heel	graze	principal	patients
chute	cord	heir	I'll	whey	rein
shoot	chord	air	isle	weigh	reign
			aisle	way	rain

1. The cows did ____**graze**____ under clouds of different colored ____**grays**____.

2. ____**I'll**____ walk down the tree-covered ____**aisle**____ on the tropical ____**isle**____.

3. I want to ____**shoot**____ your picture when you race down the water ____**chute**____.

4. When the pianist hit the song's first ____**chord**____, an electrical ____**cord**____ shorted and the concert hall went dark.

5. The doctor's ____**patients**____ had little ____**patience**____ when they learned the doctor would be an hour late.

6. We drove to our state's ____**capital**____, Springfield, Illinois, and we got a tour of the ____**capitol**____.

7. Tim ____**threw**____ a ball ____**through**____ the air for his dog to chase.

8. The prince would someday be ____**heir**____ to the throne, and he promised to clean up the polluted ____**air**____.

9. The one ____**principle**____ that the ____**principal**____ expected the students to maintain was "always do your very best, and you will feel success."

10. John had a sore on his ____**heel**____ that would not ____**heal**____.

Congratulations!

_____

receives this award for

_____

Signed _____

Date _____

adapt	admit	aquarium	ambition
anchor	assist	atmosphere	background
behavior	blizzard	brilliant	candidate
capable	celebrate	climate	colonial

© CD

chrome	concrete	deserve	detective
© CD	© CD	© CD	© CD
benefit	earnest	economy	electron
© CD	© CD	© CD	© CD
encounter	enormous	exchange	forecast
© CD	© CD	© CD	© CD
fossil	frequent	garment	gesture
© CD	© CD	© CD	© CD

glimpse

photograph

hesitate

© CD

identify

intelligence

harvest

intestines

latitude

© CD

longitude

magnificent

maintain

marvelous

© CD

autograph

museum

nucleus

numerous

© CD

orbit	organism	organize	outcome
outline	overlook	particular	patient
peculiar	natural	preserve	protect
propose	publish	recover	rejoice

remark	research	repair	reveal
telegraph	route	scarce	seldom
shield	shift	signal	slight
synonym	different	suspend	temperature

© CD

thorough	transmit	trial	underground
universal	vaccination	valuable	vessel
victory	violin	visible	volcano
voyage	opposite	wilderness	yield

© CD